Check Point Education Series

# Security Engineering Student Manual

R76 Edition

| | |
|---|---|
| International Headquarters: | 5 Ha'Solelim Street<br>Tel Aviv 67897, Israel<br>Tel: +972-3-753 4555 |
| U.S. Headquarters: | 959 Skyway Road, Suite 300<br>San Carlos, CA 94070<br>Tel: 650-628-2000 |
| Technical Support, Education & Professional Services: | 6330 Commerce Drive, Suite 120<br>Irving, TX 75063<br>Tel: 972-444-6612<br>E-mail any comments or questions about our courseware to: courseware@us.checkpoint.com.<br>For questions or comments about other Check Point documentation, e-mail: CP_TechPub_Feedback@checkpoint.com. |
| Document #: | DOC-Manual-CCSE-R76 |
| Revision: | R76.2013 |
| Content: | Mark Hoefle, Joey Witt |
| Graphics: | Chunming Jia |
| Contributors | **Beta Testing and Technical Review**<br>Chris Alblas - Arrow ECS - England<br>Eric Anderson - Netanium - United States<br>Moshe Ashkenazy - Check Point Software Technologies _ Israel<br>David Buchweitz - SecureData - South Africa<br>Kishin Fatnani - K-Secure - India<br>Doron Meidan - John Bryce Training - Israel<br>John Raymond - Wick Hill - England<br>Alejandro Diez Rodriguez - Afina - Spain<br>Gil Rozenberg - John Bryce Training - Israel<br>Saraf Shmutz - John Bryce Training - Israel<br>Erik Wagemans - JCA - Belgium<br>Tim Hall - Shasow Peak - USA<br>**Special Thanks:**<br>Oren Parnes - John Bryce Training<br>Kim Winfield - Check Point Software Technologies<br>Rob Hughes - Check Point Software Technologies<br>**Test Development:**<br>Ken Finley - Check Point<br>**Check Point Technical Publications Team:**<br>Rochelle Fisher, DalyYam, Eli Har-Even, Paul Grigg, Richard Levine, Rivkah Albinder, Shira Rosenfield, Yaakov Simon |

# Contents

Preface

# *Security Engineering*

# Introduction

Welcome to the Check Point Security Engineering course.

This course is intended to provide you with an understanding of key concepts and skills necessary to effectively build, modify, deploy and troubleshoot a network using the Check Point Security Firewall.

The *Security Engineering* course provides you with the following key elements:

- Advanced and in-depth explanation of Check Point firewall technology
- Key tips and techniques for troubleshooting the Firewall Software Blade.
- Advanced upgrading concepts and practices
- Clustering firewall, management concepts and practices
- Software acceleration features
- Advanced VPN concepts and implementations
- Reporting tools, deployment options and features

This course provides hands-on training for building and configuring a network using the Check Point Security Gateway software blade & Gaia. You will configure a Security Gateway in standalone and clustered deployments while implementing certificate-based and remote access VPNs using SmartConsole clients. You will also learn how to perform advanced troubleshooting tasks on the firewall.

## Course Design

This course is designed for expert users and resellers who need to perform advanced deployment configurations of a Security Gateway.

The following professionals benefit best from this course:

- System administrators
- Support analysts
- Network engineers

## Course Prerequisites

Successful completion of this course depends on knowledge of multiple disciplines related to network-security activities:

- UNIX and Windows operating systems
- Certificate management
- System administration
- CCSA training/certification
- Networking (TCP/IP)

## Course Chapters and Objectives

### *Chapter 1: Upgrading*

1. Perform a backup of a Security Gateway and Management Server using your understanding of the differences between backups, snapshots, and upgrade-exports.
2. Upgrade a Management Server using a database migration.

### *Chapter 2: Advanced Firewall*

1. Using your knowledge of Security Gateway infrastructure including chain modules, packet flow and kernel tables, describe how to perform debugs on firewall processes.

### *Chapter 3: Clustering and Acceleration*

1. Build, test and troubleshoot a ClusterXL Load Sharing deployment on an enterprise network.
2. Build, test and troubleshoot a ClusterXL High Availability deployment on an enterprise network.
3. Build, test and troubleshoot a management HA deployment on an enterprise network.
4. Configure, maintain and troubleshoot SecureXL and CoreXL acceleration solutions on the corporate network traffic to ensure noted performance enhancement on the firewall.
5. Build, test and troubleshoot a VRRP deployment on an enterprise network.

### *Chapter 4: Advanced User Management*

1. Using an external user database such as LDAP, configure User Directory to incorporate user information for authentication services on the network.
2. Manage internal and external user access to resources for Remote Access or across a VPN.

### *Chapter 5: Advanced IPsec VPN and Remote Access*

1. Using your knowledge of fundamental VPN tunnel concepts, troubleshoot a site-to-site or certificate-based VPN on a corporate gateway using IKEView, VPN log files and command-line debug tools.
2. Optimize VPN performance and availability by using Link Selection and Multiple Entry Point solutions.
3. Manage and test corporate VPN tunnels to allow for greater monitoring and scalability with multiple tunnels defined in a community including other VPN providers.

### *Chapter 6: Auditing and Reporting*

1. Create Events or use existing event definitions to generate reports on specific network traffic using SmartReporter and SmartEvent in order to provide industry compliance information to management.
2. Using your knowledge of SmartEvent architecture and module communication, troubleshoot report generation given command-line tools and debug-file information.

We begin our course with a study of firewall processes and procedures for Security Management Servers and Gateways. We will take a close look at user and kernel process, stateful inspection, and kernel tables, and note important troubleshooting guidelines. Take note of issues you have encountered in your experiences, and how they might have been addressed differently in your infrastructure.

Review the course topology. Note the location of each server in relation to the Gateway, and how they are routed. Make sure you understand the purpose for each server, and the credentials used for accessing each server and the applications used.

Finally, read through the chapter objectives. These guide you in understanding the purpose for the lectures and lab exercises.

## Lab Topology

This course was developed using VMware Workstation and as such all systems in the lab topology are virtual machines running on a single host machine.

Your instructor will have information as to the specific settings and configuration requirements of each virtual machine configuration, if you need them.

The lab topology is as follows:

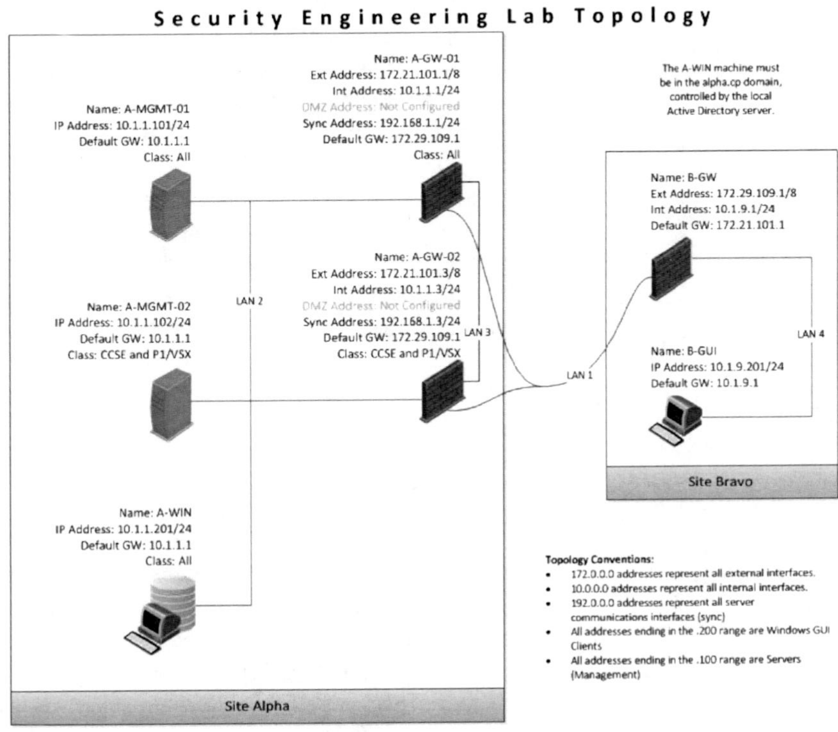


Figure 1 — Lab Topology

# Check Point 3D Security

Applying security measures to an organization's network is more than knowing how to push a policy, or building a cluster. It's about knowing how that policy is going to affect network processes, whether the policy will impede employee's ability to get their job done, or whether the redundancy is needed more for management, or a gateway. The Check Point 3D vision is about applying policies to serve business needs, while enforcing network security centrally, minimizing impact to the users. Educating company employees about the merit of upholding secure business practices is part and parcel to good enforcement, because users need the resources the network provides to do their jobs most effectively. Users become part of the process of security by learning the risks, applying safe practices depending on their role in the organization, and understanding that keeping data safe protects their jobs.

Throughout this course, keep in mind that to address the corporate policy, or to enforce changes in the corporate security infrastructure impacts employee productivity. Security should be thought of as a process, and any security measure that is implemented must take into account the needs of the individual within the context of corporate mandates.

## Security is a Process

What sets apart expert network administrators is the understanding that nothing in a network is ever 100% secure. New vulnerabilities in software become apparent daily, and security products must rush to keep pace with the ever growing threats to our data. Though product patches, upgrades, and new product releases provide some level of protection, there is a need to apply strict processes that recognize this inherent insecurity in products. Regular maintenance cycles must be implemented. Constant monitoring of evolving cyber-attacks has become almost mandatory so that attack signatures are updated.

In order to be compliant according to the highest IT security standards today, a company's IT security policies must be transparent. Transparency in information security and information technology is all about having good processes, knowing how and why they work, documenting them thoroughly, and reporting on the result.

The challenges to IT involve security, deployment, management, and finally compliance. Security is the number one concern, but though security can never be perfect, risk to your organization is still manageable.

A common way of thinking about security products is that they prevent threats to resource data. A better way to look at them is as tools to avoid risk. Threats will always exist, and more will evolve that were never considered by the code developers, simply because the potential for threats is enormous and impossible to predict. Some amount of risk is acceptable, however, and some amount is not, depending on the needs of an organization. Avoiding risk is a continuous process, or to put it another way, security processes define how an organization minimizes risk.

In the same way banking institutions conduct double audits, and provide monitoring of your ATM card, organizations can implement safeguards on network traffic by creating strategic policies and automating IT processes. By automating monitoring, enforcement, and reporting of these policies, organizations learn employee and partner behavior regarding IT assets and intellectual property. In learning how the data is used, processes can be fine-tuned to mitigate risks even further. For example, despite malware protections, an endpoint is found to be infected by a keylogger Trojan. Unless a process is put in place that isolates that endpoint from infecting an entire enterprise network, much of the corporate data is at a high risk of being stolen.

The following summarizes some guidelines to incorporating IT security best practices, which directly apply to a typical task list for a network administrator:

1. **Perform a risk assessment.** Know where your risks lie. Identify areas that show any potential for problems and assess the likelihood and level of impact accordingly.
2. **Develop and enforce a policy.** Use best practices and implement them heaviest at your most weakest point in your network. Consider the strictest enforcement at first, then apply exceptions carefully based on needs assessments and role specific guidelines in order to minimize impact to productivity.
3. **Address known vulnerabilities.** Most common vulnerabilities exist in operating systems, popular applications, Web browsers, and virtual platforms.
4. **Control and Monitor devices.** It is necessary to control what is moved on and off these devices. Monitor the devices for malicious software and provide sufficient controls to minimize impact to the corporate network in the event that safeguards don't succeed. Also, decide what personnel or processes must be involved for the control to be implemented successfully.
5. **Conduct audits.** Periodic audits provide useful insight into the effectiveness of the policies and enforcement measures. Adjustments to the policies are made more effective by this insight, and should be part of the necessary maintenance process.

# *Deployment Scenario*

For this course, assume you are a network administrator for a company called, Alpha Corp. which provides out-sourced customer contact management solutions for a wide range of call center services. The company employs about 2,000 employees worldwide, maintaining key departments in finance, human resources, MIS, products, sales and corporate development.

All of the major departments are located at headquarters, and some sales staff, technical support, MIS and data center personnel are located at the branch offices - Bravo. A corporate firewall is already implemented. You have a dedicated server installed for the management, and SmartConsole clients running on a separate endpoint.

In addition, you have remote users employed by Alpha Corp., i.e., sales staff and technical services personnel that need to connect via VPN to headquarters:

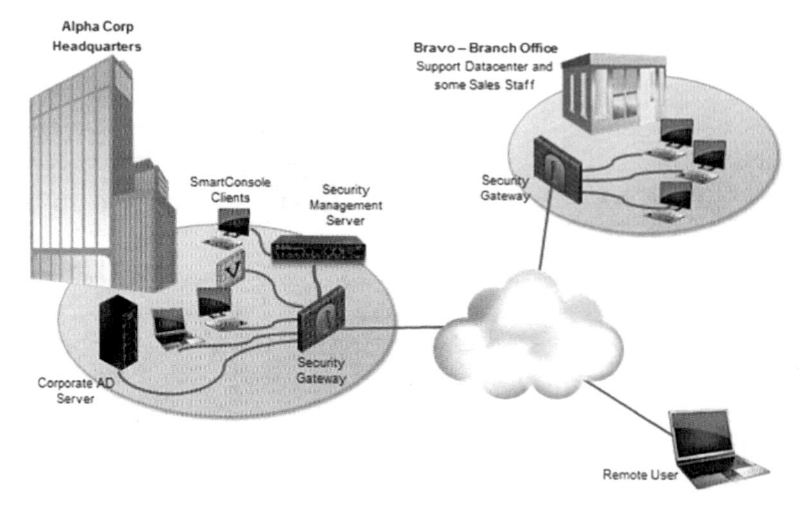


Figure 2 — Alpha Corp

# CHAPTER 1 Upgrading

# *Upgrading*

Upgrades are used to save Check Point product configurations, Security Policies, and objects, so that Security Administrators do not need to re-create Gateway and Security Management Server configurations.

## Chapter Objectives:

- Perform a backup of a Security Gateway and Management Server using your understanding of the differences between backups, snapshots, and upgrade-exports.
- Upgrade and troubleshoot a Management Server using a database migration.

# Back up and Restore Security Gateways and Management Servers

Check Point provides three methods for backing up and restoring the operating system and networking parameters on open servers and appliances.

- Snapshot and Revert
- Backup and Restore
- upgrade_export/ migrate export

Each of these methods backs up certain parameters and has relative advantages and disadvantages (i.e. file size, speed, and portability).

## Snapshot Image Management

Before performing an upgrade, you can use the command line to create a Snapshot image of the OS, or of the packages distributed. If the upgrade or distribution operation fails, you can use the command line to revert the disk to the saved image.

### *Gaia Snapshot Image Management*

With Gaia snapshot image management you can:

- Make a new image (a snapshot) of the system. You can revert to the image at a later time.
- Revert to a locally stored image. This restores the system, including configuration of installed products.
- Delete an image from the local system.
- Export an existing image. This creates a compressed version of the image. You can then download the exported image to another computer and delete the exported image from the original computer, to save disk space.
- Import uploads an exported image and makes an image of it (a snapshot). You can revert to the image at a later time.
- View a list of images that are stored locally.

## Upgrade Tools

The upgrade tools backs up all Check Point configurations, independent of hardware, operating system and Check Point version. Use this utility to backup Check Point configuration settings on the management station. The migrate utility is intended for upgrades or migration of database information to new systems with hardware changes, and will not work when downgrading to an earlier Check Point version. The file size is smaller and depends on the size of your policy. Assuming the CPU on the machine is not over-loaded, it can be initiated on a live system without interrupting services.

## Backup Schedule Recommendations

Perform backups using any of the methods described during maintenance windows to limit disruptions to services, CPU utilization, and time allotment.

- **Snapshot** — Perform snapshots at least once or before major changes, such as upgrades.
- **Backup** — Perform a backup every couple of months, depending on how frequently changes are made to the network or policy.
- **Upgrade_export/migrate export** — Export at least every month depending on changes to the network or policy, and before an upgrade or migration. This method can be performed anytime outside a maintenance window.

Test your backups with either the backup, upgrade_export, or migrate export files.

## Upgrade Tools

Before you upgrade appliances or computers, make use of the appropriate Check Point upgrade tools. There is a different package of tools for each platform. (After installation, you can find the upgrade tools in the installation directory).

| Upgrade Tools Packages | Description |
|---|---|
| migrate.conf | For an Advanced Upgrade (migration of Security Management Server database) or a Security Management Server to Multi-Domain Server migration, this file is necessary. |
| migrate | Runs Advanced Upgrade or migration.<br>On Windows, this is migrate.exe. |

TABLE 1: Upgrade Tool Packages

| Upgrade Tools Packages | Description |
| --- | --- |
| pre_upgrade_verifier.exe | Analyzes compatibility of the currently installed configuration with the upgrade version. It gives a report on the actions to take before and after the upgrade. |
| upgrade_export | Backs up all Check Point configurations, without operating system information. On Windows, this is upgrade_export.exe. |
| upgrade_import | Restores backed up configuration. On Windows, this is upgrade_import.exe. |
| cp_merge | Used to export and import policy packages, and merge objects from a given file into the Security Management server database. |

TABLE 1: Upgrade Tool Packages

## Performing Upgrades

As in all upgrade procedures, first upgrade your Security Management Server or Multi-Domain Server before upgrading the gateways. Once the management has been successfully upgraded and contains a contract file, the contract file is transferred to a gateway when the gateway is upgraded (the contract file is retrieved from the management).

## Support Contract

Before upgrading a gateway or Security Management server, you need to have a valid support contract that includes software upgrade and major releases registered to your Check Point User Center account. The contract file is stored on Security Management server and downloaded to security gateways during the upgrade process. By verifying your status with the User Center, the contract file enables you to easily remain compliant with current Check Point licensing standards.

### *On Gaia, SecurePlatform and Windows*

When upgrading Security Management server, the upgrade process checks to see whether a contract file is already present on the server. If not, the main options for obtaining a contract are displayed. You can download a contract file or import it.

If the contract file does not cover the Security Management server, a message on Download or Import informs you that the Security Management server is not eligible for upgrade. The absence of a valid contract file does not prevent upgrade. You can download a valid contract at a later date using SmartUpdate.

### *On Security Gateways*

You can upgrade Security Gateways using one of these methods:

- **SmartUpdate** — Centrally upgrade and manage Check Point software and licenses from a SmartConsole client.
- **Local Upgrade** — Do a local upgrade on the Security Gateway itself.

After you accept the End User License Agreement (EULA), the upgrade process searches for a valid contract on the gateway. If a valid contract is not located, the upgrade process attempts to retrieve the latest contract file from the Security Management server. If not found, you can download or import a contract.

If the contract file does not cover the gateway, a message informs you (on Download or Import) that the gateway is not eligible for upgrade. The absence of a valid contract file does not prevent upgrade. When the upgrade is complete, contact your local support provider to obtain a valid contract. Use SmartUpdate to install the contract file.

Use the download or import instructions for installing a contract file on a Security Management Server.

If you continue without a contract, you can install a valid contract file later. But the gateway is not eligible for upgrade. You may be in violation of your Check Point Licensing Agreement, as shown in the final message of the upgrade process. In such cases, contact your reseller.

### *Upgrading the Security Management Server*

You do not have to upgrade the Security Management server and all of the gateways at the same time. When the Security Management server is upgraded, you can still manage gateways from earlier versions (though the gateways may not support new features).

> **Note:** **Important** - To upgrade, make sure there is enough free disk space in /var/log.

Use the Pre-Upgrade Verification Tool to reduce the risk of incompatibility with your existing environment. The Pre-Upgrade Verification Tool generates a detailed report of the actions to take before an upgrade.

There are different upgrade methods for the Security Management server:

- Upgrade Production Security Management server
- Migrate and Upgrade to a New Security Management server

**Note:** **Important** - After upgrade, you cannot restore a version with a database revision that was made with the old version. You can see old version database saves in Read-Only mode.

# Upgrading Standalone Full High Availability

**Full High Availability** — The server and the gateway are in a standalone configuration and each has High Availability to a second standalone machine. If there is a failure, the server and the gateway failover to the secondary machine.

In the standalone configuration the server and gateway can failover independently of each other. For example, if only the server has an issue, only that server fails over. There is no effect on the gateway in the standalone configuration.

To upgrade Full High Availability for cluster members in standalone configurations, there are different options:

- Upgrade one machine and synchronize the second machine with minimal downtime.
- Upgrade with a clean installation on one machine and synchronize the second machine with system downtime.

## *Minimal Effort Upgrade*

This upgrade method to a cluster treats each individual cluster member as an individual gateway, assuming network downtime is permitted. In this case, follow the same procedure for each gateway cluster member for upgrading as you would for a distributed deployment scenario.

## *Upgrading with Minimal Downtime*

You can do a Full High Availability upgrade with minimal downtime to the cluster members.

To upgrade Full High Availability with minimal downtime:

1. Make sure the primary cluster member is active and the secondary is standby: check the status of the members.
2. Start failover to the second cluster member. The secondary cluster member processes all the traffic.
3. Log in with SmartDashboard to the management server of the secondary cluster member.
4. Click Change to Active.
5. Configure the secondary cluster member to be the active management server.

    **Note:** We recommend to export the database using the Upgrade tools.

6. Upgrade the primary cluster member to the appropriate version.
7. Log in with SmartDashboard to the management server of the primary cluster member. Make sure version of the SmartDashboard is the same as the server.
8. Upgrade the version of the object to the new version.
9. Install the policy on the cluster object. The primary cluster member processes all the traffic.

   **Note:** Make sure that the For Gateway Clusters install on all the members option is cleared. Selecting this option causes the installation to fail.

10. Upgrade the secondary cluster member to the appropriate version.
11. Synchronize for management High Availability.

You can also do a Full High Availability upgrade with a clean installation on the secondary cluster member and synchronize the primary cluster member. This type of upgrade causes downtime to the cluster members.

Best practice: If the appliance to upgrade is the primary member of a cluster, export its database before you upgrade.

# Practice and Review

## Practice Lab

Lab 1: Upgrading to Check Point R76

## Review Questions

1. When should snapshots be performed?

2. To run advanced upgrade or migration, what tool is used?

3. What is a critical task for both Snapshots and Backups?

CHAPTER 2

# *Advanced Firewall*

# Advanced Firewall

The Check Point Firewall Software Blade builds on the award-winning technology, first offered in Check Point's firewall solution, to provide the industry's best gateway security with identity awareness. Check Point's firewalls are trusted by 100% of Fortune 100 companies and deployed by over 170,000 customers. Check Point products have demonstrated industry leadership and continued innovation since the introduction of FireWall-1 in 1994.

## Chapter Objectives:

- Using knowledge of Security Gateway infrastructure, including chain modules, packet flow and kernel tables to describe how to perform debugs on firewall processes.

# Check Point Firewall Infrastructure

As a security expert considering the needs of your organization, you must apply in-depth knowledge of security gateways as you implement them beyond a simple distributed deployment. In order to establish a good framework for troubleshooting gateways in a complex network topology, you must fully understand the  infrastructure.

You should recall that fundamentally, Check Point security components are divided into the following components:

- GUI clients
- Security Management
- Security Gateway

## GUI Clients

SmartConsole applications, such as SmartView Tracker, SmartEvent, SmartReporter and SmartDashboard are executable files available for Windows operating systems. These GUI applications offer the administrator the ability to configure, manage and monitor security solutions, perform maintenance tasks, generate reports and enforce corporate policy in real-time.

Check Point periodically releases new executables that include updates for these applications, also known as "GUI HFAs". These, however, are not related or aligned with Security Gateway HFAs and are considered a separate, unrelated release track.

## Management

The management component is responsible for all management operations in the system. It contains several different components, such as the management, reporting suite, log server, etc. All of the functionality of the management server is implemented in User-Mode processes, where each process is responsible for several operations. The most significant processes are:

- FWM
- FWD
- CPD
- CPWD (Check Point WatchDog)

## *Security Gateway*

The Security Gateway, usually referred to simply as the "Firewall," is the component in the system responsible for security enforcement, encryption/decryption, authentication and accounting.

The functionality of the security gateway is implemented both in User-Mode and in the Kernel. As the security gateway is first and foremost a network device running an OS, it is inherently vulnerable to various network layer attacks. To mitigate this risk and others, some of the firewall functionality is implemented in the OS kernel. This allows the traffic to be inspected before even getting to the OS IP stack.

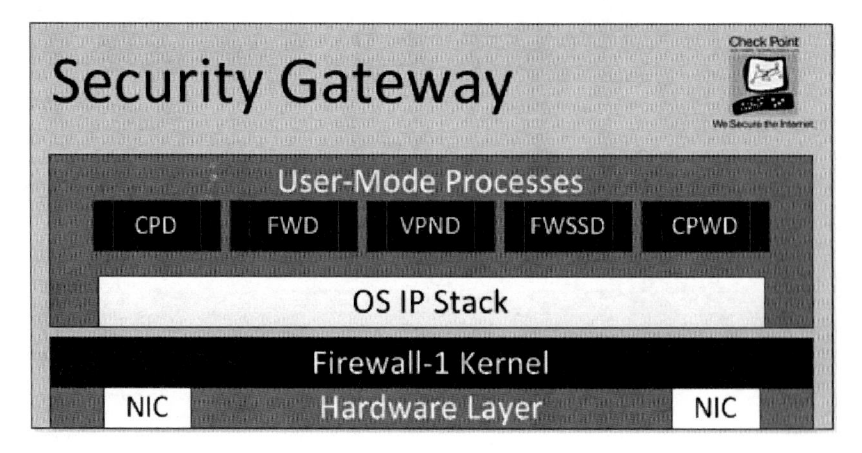


Figure 3 — OS Kernel

## User and Kernel Mode Processes

As administrators trying to debug the firewall, the first observation to make is to decide which Firewall functionality is implemented in the user space and which is implemented in the kernel. Once you make that distinction, you can decide the best approach to addressing the problem, including which tool is the most appropriate to use.

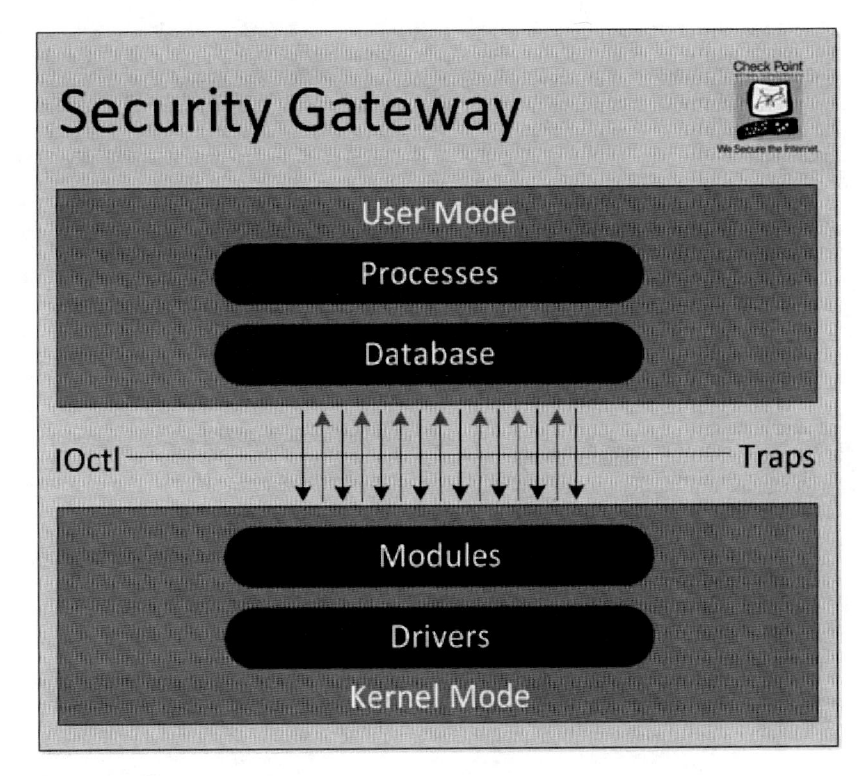


Figure 4 — Processes

The firewall kernel is responsible for the majority of the security gateway's operations, such as security enforcement, encryption/decryption NAT, etc. In order to detect which part of the kernel might be responsible for a specific issue, start by considering the inner structure of the FW kernel and it's interaction with the OS kernel, the hardware, and other kernel components, such as acceleration.

The Kernel mode resides in the lowest possible location. Every packet that goes through the FW is inspected. Whereas in the Network layers, you would not see all those packets.

The User Mode is actually not mandatory, but it allows the FW to function more efficiently in the application layer. The FW employs services that the OS provides and allows easier inspection of files on open connections.

It is possible and, in some cases, required for user and kernel processes to communicate. To allow this, there are two mechanisms: IOctl (Input/Output Controls) and traps. When a kernel process wishes to signal to a user mode process it sets a "trap", i.e., changes a value in a registry key. The user mode process monitoring that flag "stumbles" on the trap and performs the requested operation. When a user mode entity needs to write information to a kernel process, it uses IOctl, which is an infrastructure allowing the entity to call a function in the kernel and supply the required parameters.

## The CPD Core Process

Check Point Daemon (CPD) is a core process available on every Check Point product. Among other things it allows the following:

1. Secure Internal Communication (SIC) functionality – Ports 18xxx are used for this communication.
2. Status – Pull AMON status from the GW/Management using SmartEvent.
3. Transferring messages between FW-1 processes.
4. Policy installation – Receives the policy (on the GW) and pushes it forward to relevant processes and the Kernel.

## fwm

**fwm** is available on any management product, including Multi-Domain Security Management, and on products that require direct GUI access, such as SmartEvent:

- GUI Client communication — This is communication between the Management Server and the GUI client.
- DB manipulation — This includes all actions that are performed on the MGMT, such as object creation, rules, and users.
- Policy compilation — **fwm** handles the policy compilation that is later applied to network traffic during the inspection process.
- Management HA sync — The sync management is handled in Management High Availability.

## fwn

**fwd** allows other processes including the kernel to forward logs to external log servers as well as the Security Management Server. It is related to policy installation and also used to communicate with the kernel using command line tools such as the fw commands; for example, when setting kernel variables or using kernel control commands

## fwssd

**fwssd** is a child process of **fwd** responsible for maintaining the Security Management Servers. Each Security Management Server will be invoked according to activated features, such as DLP, and corresponding rules with URI resource, SMTP resource, and authentication. The processes that actually run as the security servers are "in.xxxx".

## cpwd

**cpwd** (also known as WatchDog) is a process that invokes and monitors critical processes such as Check Point daemons on the local machine, and attempts to restart them if they fail. Among the processes monitored by Watchdog are cpd, **fwd**, **fwm**. The **cpwd_admin** utility is used to show the status of processes, and to configure **cpwd**.

## Inbound and Outbound Packet Flow

These processes work on each packet through another process called inspection. To understand how the packets are inspected, consider the firewall kernel more closely. The firewall's kernel consists of two completely separate logical parts called the "Inbound" and "Outbound" representing the process of a packet coming into and out from the firewall (respectively):

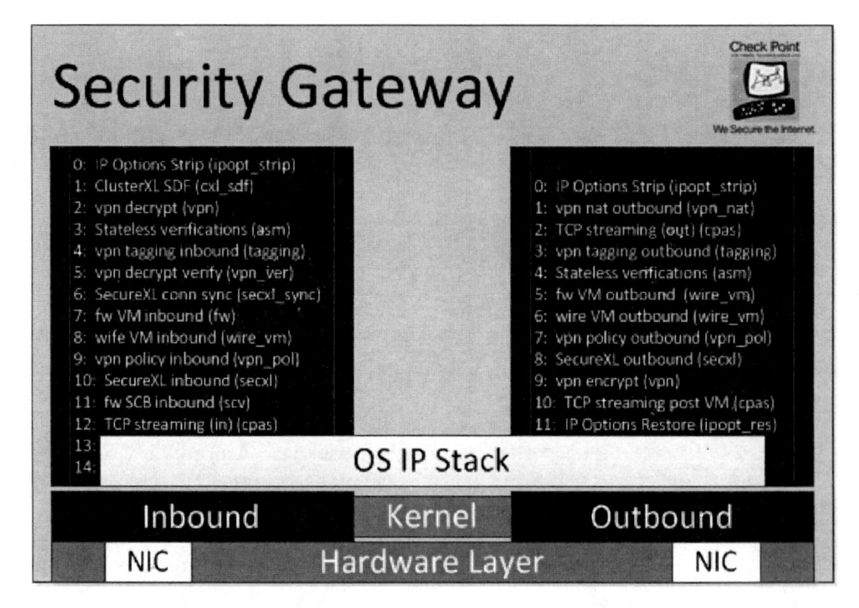


Figure 5 — Firewall Kernel

Each part of the kernel acts independent and does not assume that a packet was inspected or processed by the other. So, some functionality is implemented both on the inbound and on the outbound. Some key points include:

- Each direction has its own ordered chain of modules (packet processing handlers).
- Handlers decide whether to continue, terminate or hold the processing of a packet.
- Inspection is performed on virtually defragmented packets.

The inspection process does expect that a packet in the outbound that hasn't visited the inbound first originated from the gateway itself. It is also assumed that a packet not originating from the gateway was inbound.

## Inbound fw ctl Chain Modules

In the following example, the chain modules are displayed:

```
in chain (16):
0: -7ffffff0 (c36aa9f0) (00000001)        tcpt inbound (tcp_tun_
1: -7f800000 (c1a32b90) (ffffffff)        IP Options Strip (in) (ipopt_strip)
2: - 2000000 (c3696c80) (00000003)        vpn decrypt (vpn)
3: - 1ffffff8 (c36a34a0) (00000001)       12tp inbound (12tp)
4: - 1ffffff6 (c1a33f60) (00000001)       Stateless verifications (in) (asm)
5: - 1ffffff2 (c36bf000) (00000003)       vpn tagging inbound (tagging)
6: - 1ffffff0 (c3697a70) (00000003)       vpn decrypt verify (vpn_ver)
7: 0 (c19e8640) (00000001)                fw VM inbound (fw)
8: 1 (c1a4b480) (00000002)                wire VM inbound (wire_vm)
9: 2000000 (c3699f40) (00000003)          vpn policy inbound (vpn_pol)
10: 21500000 (c4b64940) (00000001)        RTM packet in (rtm)
11: 7f600000 (c1a29880) (00000001)        fw SCV inbound (scv)
12: 7f730000 (c1b61200) (00000001)        passive streaming (in) (pass_str)
13: 7f750000 (c1c73910) (00000001)        TCP streaming (in) (cpas)
14: 7f800000 (c1a32f20) (ffffffff)        IP Options Restore (in) (ipopt_res)
15: 7fb00000 (c1c3f260) (00000001)        HA Forwarding (ha_for)
```

Figure 6 — Inbound Chain

In this figure, we see the inbound chain, though this is just one example and in different configurations some chain modules will not appear and others might be added.

Between different releases, we sometimes add or completely remove chain modules, depending on the version specific design decisions.

## Outbound Chain Modules

In the following example, chain modules are displayed:

```
out chain (15):
0: -7f800000 (c1a32b90) (ffffffff)          IP Options Strip (out) (ipopt_strip)
1: - 1ffffff (c3698b20) (00000003)          vpn nat outbound (vpn_nat)
2: - 1fffff0 (c1c73790) (00000001)          TCP streaming (out) (cpas)
3 -  1ffff50 (c1b61200) (00000001)          passive streaming (out) (pass_str)
4: - 1ff0000 (c36bf000) (00000003)          vpn tagging outbound (tagging)
5: - 1f00000 (c1a33f60) (00000001)          Stateless verifications (out) (asm)
6: 0 (c19e8640) (00000001)                  fw VM outbound (fw)
7: 1 (c1a4b480) (00000002)                  wire VM outbound (wire_vm)
8: 2000000 (c36999f0) (00000003)            vpn policy outbound (vpn_pol)
9: 1ffffff0 (c36a3130) (00000001)           12tp outbound (12tp)
10: 20000000 (c3698d90) (00000003)          vpn encrypt (vpn)
11: 24000000 (c4b64940) (00000001)          RTM packet out (rtm)
12: 60000000 (c36aac50) (00000001)          tcpt outbound (tcp_tun)
13: 7f700000 (c1c73530) (00000001)          TCP streaming post VM (cpas)
14: 7f800000 (c1a32f20) (ffffffff)          IP Options Restore (ipopt_res)
```

Figure 7 — Outbound Chain

Shown in this figure, the outbound chain shows roughly the same chain modules as seen on the inbound. The most significant difference is that in the inbound, the vpn decrypt and vpn decrypt verify chain modules are seen. This makes sense because you would expect a packet to be decrypted on the inbound. In addition, the outbound chain also has the vpn encrypt chain module in case the packet needs to be encrypted on the outbound.

## Columns in a Chain

Consider the following chain example:

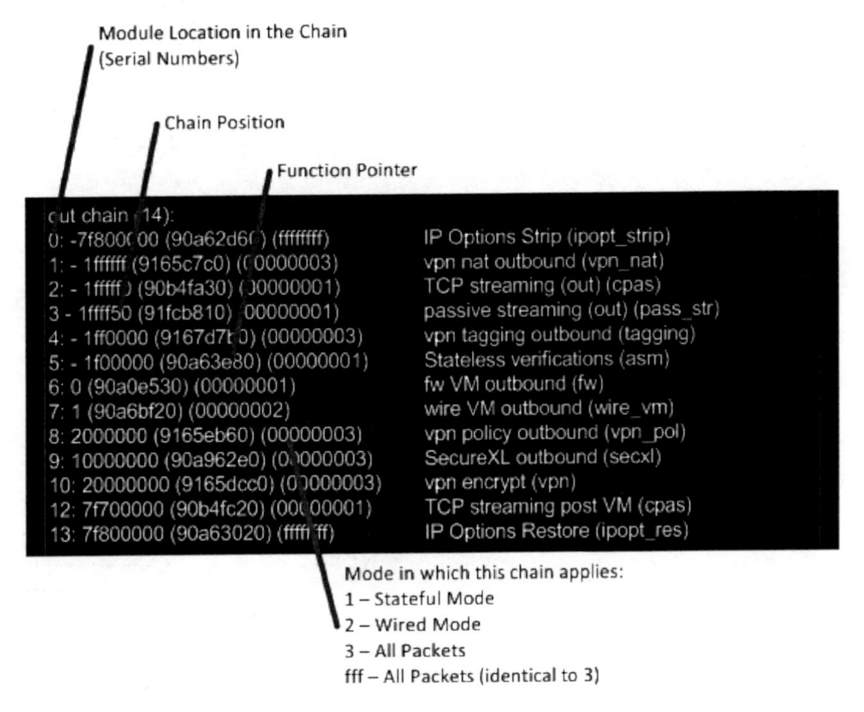


Figure 8 — Location of Modules in the Chain

The location of the module in the chain is a relative, serial number to the location of this chain module for this particular gateway configuration. For example, as in the above the "fw VM outbound" is the 6th chain module. It might be in a different location in other gateway scenarios.

The chain position is an absolute number that never changes.

In the VPN chapter, we will learn that in wire mode we do not want the firewall to enforce stateful features on a packet. To address concerns such as this, in the firewall kernel each kernel chain is associated with a key. This key specifies the type of traffic applicable to this chain module. For wire-mode configuration, chain modules marked with "1" will not apply and for stateful mode, the chain modules marked with "2" will not apply. Chain modules marked with "fff…" (IP options strip/restore) and "3" will apply to all traffic. To try this on a firewall in your lab, run the following command:

**fw ctl chain**

## Stateful Inspection

Stateful Inspection was invented by Check Point, providing accurate and highly efficient traffic inspection. It implements all necessary firewall capabilities between the Data and Network layers (layers 2 and 3), but is capable of processing data from layers 4-7 for improved security.

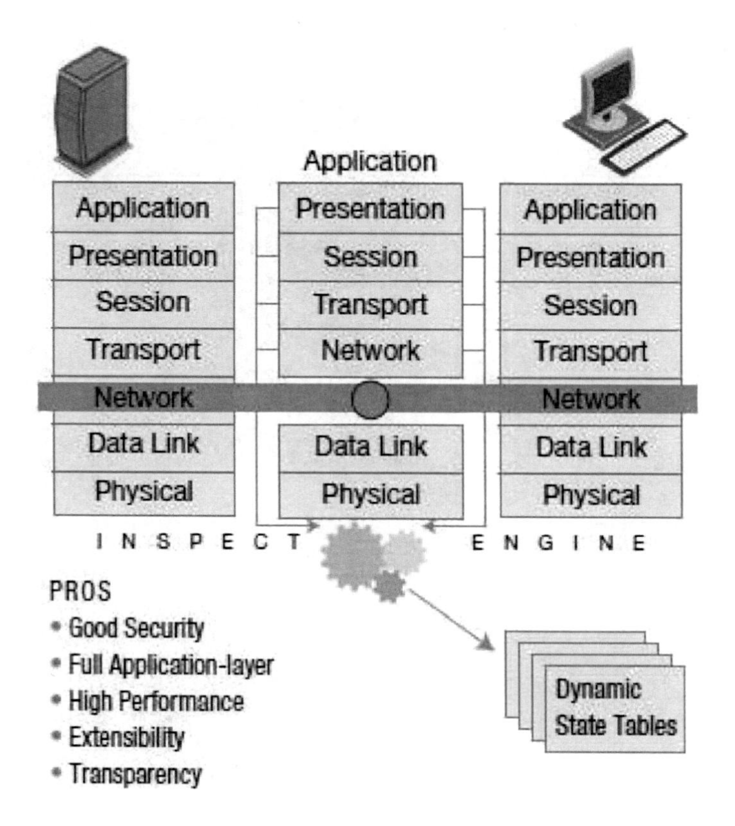


Figure 9 — Stateful Inspection

The inspection engine examines every packet as they are intercepted at the Network layer. The connection state and context information are stored and updated dynamically in the kernel tables.

To see the process flow of the inspection engine, review the flow chart below:

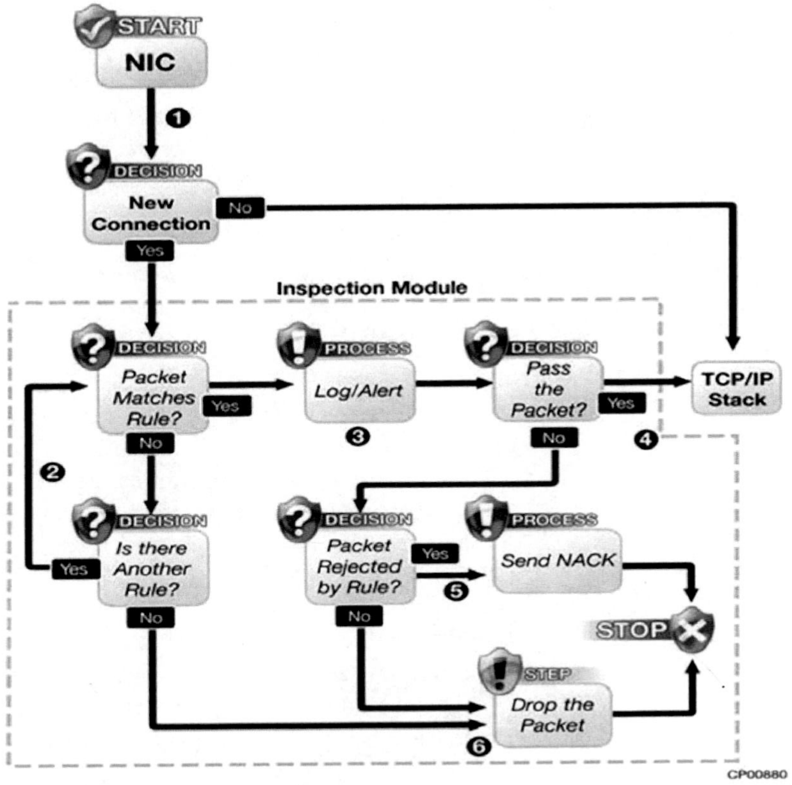

Figure 10 — Inspection Module

1. Packets pass through the NIC to the Inspection Module. The Inspection Module inspects the packets and their data.
2. Packets are matched to the policy rule base, one rule at a time. Packets that do not match any rule are dropped.
3. Logging and/or alerts that have been defined are activated.
4. Packets that pass inspection are moved through the TCP/IP stack to their destination.
5. For packets that do not pass inspection and are rejected by the rule definition, an acknowledgment is sent (i.e., RST packet on TCP, and ICMP unreachable on UDP).
6. The packets that do not pass inspection and do not apply to any of the rules, are dropped without sending a negative acknowledgment.

# *Kernel Tables*

There are dozens of Kernel tables, each storing information relevant to a specific firewall function. Using the information saved in the Kernel tables, very elaborate and precise protections can be implemented. To view all the existing Kernel tables, type the command **fw tab -t** ***<tablename>*** at the command prompt. To view only the table names and get a perspective on the number of Kernel tables available, on SecurePlatform/Gaia use the following command:

**fw tab | grep -e "----" | more**

or

**fw tab -s**

> **Note:** To view the tables in coreXL, use the following instead of the **fw tab - t** shown above: **-i #core_number**

Most of the traffic related information is saved in the Kernel tables. (There is also information stored in **htabs**, **ghtabs**, arrays, **kbufs**, and other devices.) Tables, however, may be created, deleted, modified and read. In particular, consider the Connections table.

The connections table is essentially an approved-connections list. The firewall, as a network security device, inspects every packet coming in and out of each interface. After the first packet is matched against the rule base, we need to assume that the returning packet might not be accepted in the rule base.

Let's discuss this scenario. Say that we allow 10.10.10.10 to browse to 10.10.10.20 via HTTP in the rule base and drop everything else. The syn packet will match the rule base and pass, but as the Syn-Ack packet comes back with the reversed tuple (source IP 10.10.10.20, Destination IP 10.10.10.10) and source port 80 with a "random" destination port.

To mitigate this, for every recorded connection, a matching, reversed - tuple entry is also added to the list of approved connections. Some scenarios such as NAT, data connections and elaborate protocols, such as VoIP, introduce more complexity to the logic behind maintaining the connections table.

## Connections Table

To understand more about how the connections table works, let's consider its important features:

- Enhanced performance
  As we saw in the INSPECT module flowchart, the action of matching a packet against the rule base may be very costly (especially if there is a very large rule base with dynamic objects and logical servers that need to be resolved). By maintaining the list of approved connections in the connections table, not every packet is matched against the rule base, thus saving valuable time and computing power.

- Allow server replies
  We noted earlier that sometimes Server to Client packets might not match the rulebase. In these cases, they would be handled by the connections table.

- Stateful Features

  - Streaming based applications (Web security, etc.)
  - Sequence verification and translation
  - Hide NAT (when the Server to Client packets returning to the firewall might not match the rulebase, need to add explicit entries to the connections table).
  - Logging, accounting, monitoring, etc.
  - Client and server identification
  - Data connections

## Connections Table Format

Each new packet is recorded in the table in all available entries. In FireWall-1 version 4.1, only one entry was made to each new connection. Each packet had to go through the connections table several times to verify all available types of connection. Today, each packet goes through a single lookup as all available entries are already recorded in the table.

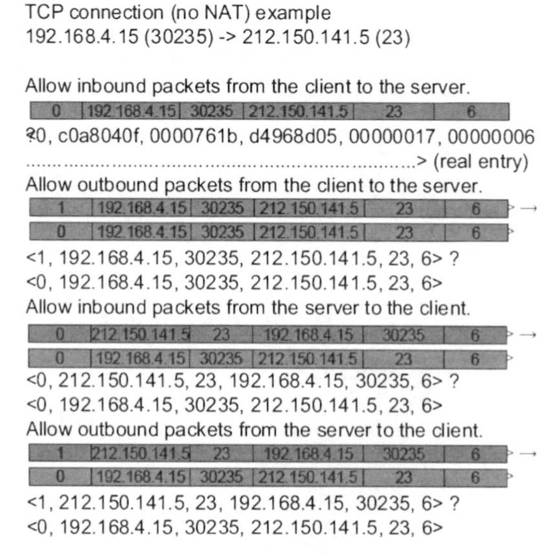

TCP connection (no NAT) example
192.168.4.15 (30235) -> 212.150.141.5 (23)
Allow inbound packets from the client to the server.
0 | 192.168.4.15 | 30235 | 212.150.141.5 | 23 | 6
<0, c0a8040f, 0000761b, d4968d05, 00000017, 00000006
........................................................................> (real entry)
Allow outbound packets from the client to the server.
1 | 192.168.4.15 | 30235 | 212.150.141.5 | 23 | 6
0 | 192.168.4.15 | 30235 | 212.150.141.5 | 23 | 6
<1, 192.168.4.15, 30235, 212.150.141.5, 23, 6> ?
<0, 192.168.4.15, 30235, 212.150.141.5, 23, 6>
Allow inbound packets from the server to the client.
0 | 212.150.141.5 | 23 | 192.168.4.15 | 30235 | 6
0 | 192.168.4.15 | 30235 | 212.150.141.5 | 23 | 6
<0, 212.150.141.5, 23, 192.168.4.15, 30235, 6> ?
<0, 192.168.4.15, 30235, 212.150.141.5, 23, 6>
Allow outbound packets from the server to the client.
1 | 212.150.141.5 | 23 | 192.168.4.15 | 30235 | 6
0 | 192.168.4.15 | 30235 | 212.150.141.5 | 23 | 6
<1, 212.150.141.5, 23, 192.168.4.15, 30235, 6> ?
<0, 192.168.4.15, 30235, 212.150.141.5, 23, 6>


Figure 11 — Connections Table

The symbolic link format provides the "6-tuple" of the connection we want to pass, and the arrow is a pointer to the tuple of the real entry in the connection table. The first 6 attributes in every entry in the connections table state the connection's "6 tuple". The 6-tuple is a unique identification of the connection within the system. The **direction** can be either "0" for Inbound or "1" for Outbound.

In the above slide, we see a simple connection representation in the connections table. The first entry is the "Real Entry", this entry holds all of the relevant information for that traffic, such as state, sequence numbers, matching rule and so on. The entry allows the Client to Server (C2S) packet to enter the firewall on the inbound. The second entry is a symbolic link, allowing for the same packets (C2S) to enter the firewall on the outbound. The third entry is another symbolic link, allowing for the Server to Client (S2C) traffic to enter the firewall on the inbound. The last entry is also a symbolic link, allowing for the S2C packet to enter the firewall on the outbound.

# *Check Point Firewall Key Features*

Before considering to debug firewall issues, let's take a closer look at firewall features that require some understanding. We've briefly touched on a few of these already, but we won't cover all of them in depth in this chapter.

The Check Point Firewall Software Blade Key Features includes:

- Packet Inspection Flow
- CoreXL (to be covered in detail in a later chapter)
- Policy Installation
- Network Address Translation
- Security Servers

## Packet Inspection Flow

Let's take a closer look at packet flow through the firewall kernel and examine how the user-mode processes work to control the traffic:

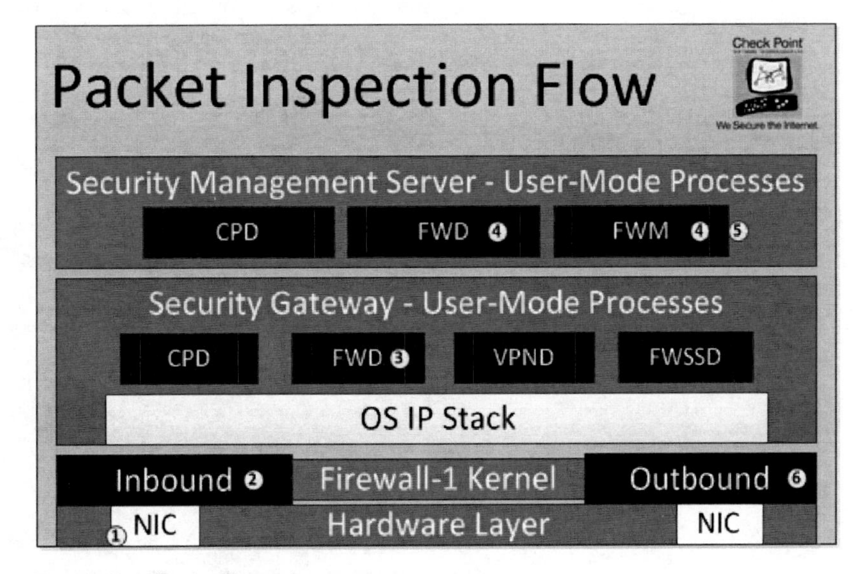


Figure 12 — Packet Inspection

1. The packet arrives at the Security Gateway, intercepted by the NIC on the inbound.
2. The firewall kernel inbound chain begins inspecting the packet.
3. Once the packet is matched against the rule base, a log is generated and sent from the kernel to the user-mode process, FWD, located in the Security Gateway.
4. The FWD process on the Security Gateway, sends the log to FWD on the Management Server, where it is forwarded to FWM via CPD.
5. FWM sends the log to the relevant SmartConsole application, such as SmartView Tracker.
6. At the same time, depending on routing decisions made by the OS, except for specific scenarios such as VPN routing, the packet is routed to a selected NIC. But the packet must go through the Firewall kernel again, only this time through the outbound chain to the appropriate NIC and to the network.

## Policy Installation Flow

The graphic displays a general process flow for Policy installation, differences are version specific, so $FWDIR is replaced with the compatibility package when other products or versions are used.

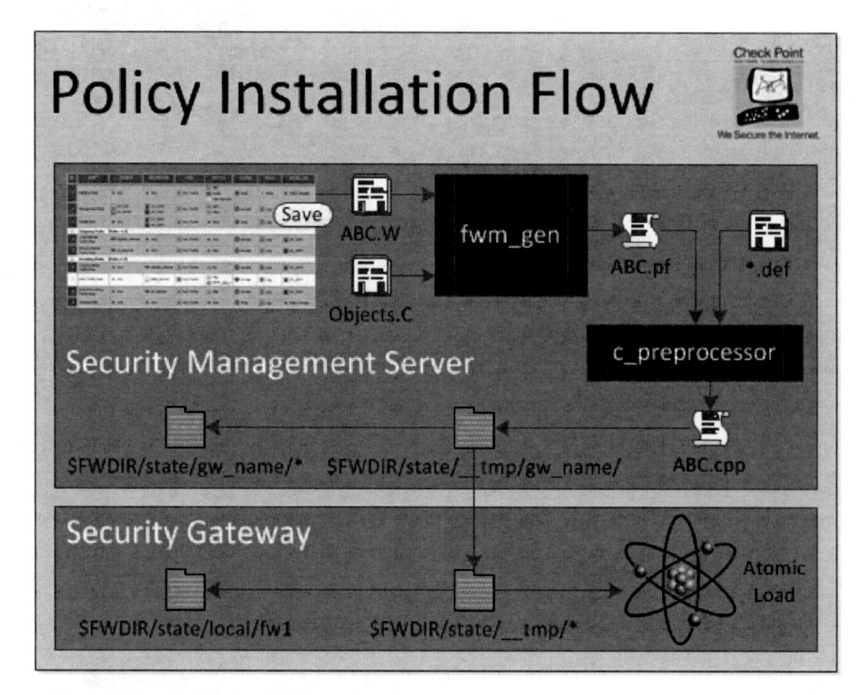


Figure 13 — Policy Installation

1. The policy is defined in the SmartDashboard GUI, i.e., in the **Firewall** tab.
2. When the policy is saved, a new file is created called **$FWDIR/conf/*.W**.

   All the ***.W** files are stored in the **rulebases_5_0.fws** location.
3. **fwm_gen** compiles the **$FWDIR/conf/*.W** into a machine language creating a new file called **$FWDIR/conf/*.pf**.

   The **$FWDIR/conf/*.pf** is actually the input from the **$FWDIR/conf/*.W** and the **$FWDIR/conf/objects.C** file.

   The **$FWDIR/conf/*.W** file is actually the exact same information defined in the GUI, just in a text format instead of a graphic one.

   The **objects.C** file contains information relevant to the policy installation only, whereas the **objects_5_0.C** includes all the objects defined in the GUI.

   **$FWDIR/conf/objects_5_0.C** is stored on the Management Server, and is important only to the Management Server.

   **$FWDIR/database/objects.C** is relevant only to the Gateway.

## Policy Installation Process

The process can be described as follows:

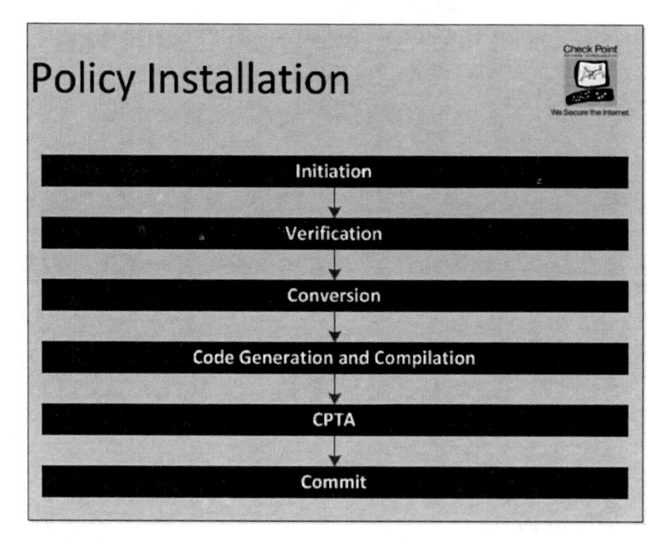


Figure 14 — Policy Installation Process

- **Initiation** — Policy installation is initiated by the GUI or from the command line. Information required for the policy installation is provided, such as the list of gateways on which the policy is to be installed.
- **Verification** — The information in the database is verified to comply with a number of rules specific to the application and package, for which policy installation is requested. If this verification fails, the process ends here, and an error message is passed to the initiator. The system can also issue warnings, in addition to fail/success messages.
- **Conversion** — The information in the database is converted from its initial format to the format understandable by later participants in the flow, such as code generation and gateway.
- **Code generation and compilation** — Policy is translated to the INSPECT language and compiled with the INSPECT compiler. Also, some additional data transformations are completed.
- **CPTA** — The Check Point Policy Transfer Agent transfers the Policy to the firewall gateway using SIC.
- **Commit** — The Gateway is instructed to load the new policy.

## Policy Installation Process Flow

Going back to the kernel, let's examine how policy installation is handled by the User-Mode processes.

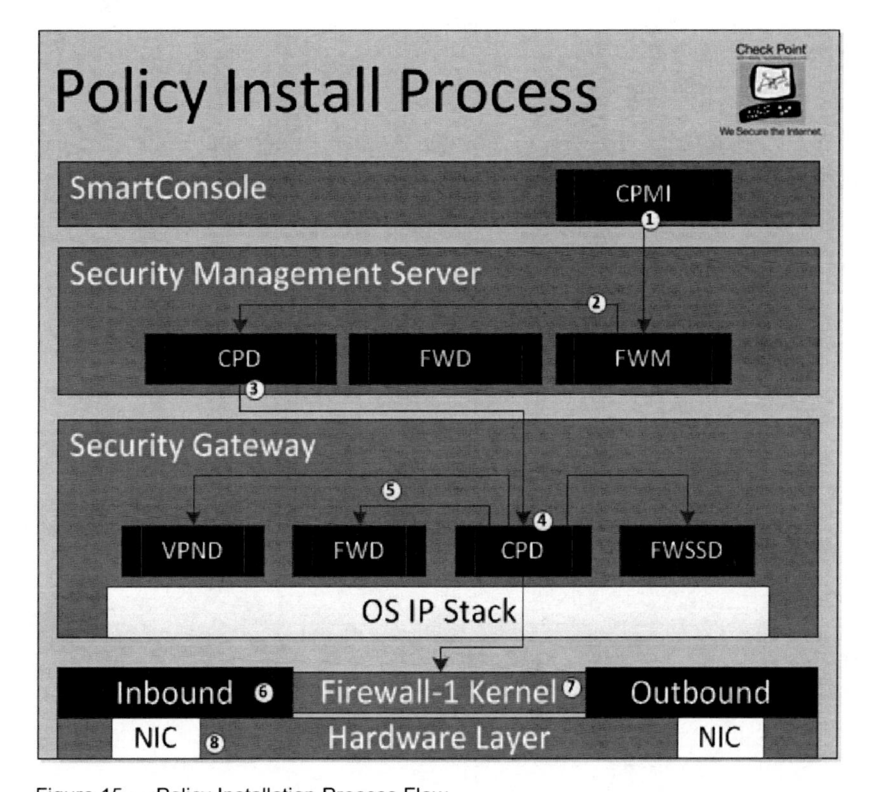


Figure 15 — Policy Installation Process Flow

1. Assuming the initiation was made by a SmartConsole application, as opposed to using command line options such as **fwm load** or **fw fetch**, the Check Point Management Interface (CPMI) policy installation command is sent to FWM on the Management Server where the verification and compilation takes place.
2. FWM forwards the command to CPD for code generation and compilation.
3. CPD invokes the Check Point Policy Transfer Agent (CPTA) command which sends the policy to all applicable Security Gateways.
4. CPD on the Security Gateway receives the policy and verifies it's integrity.
5. CPD on the Gateway updates all of the user-mode processes responsible for enforcement aspects. These include VPND for VPN issues, FWSSD processes for security server issues and so on. Once complete, the CPD then initiates the kernel replacement.
6. The new policy is prepared, and the kernel halts the traffic and starts queuing all incoming traffic.
7. The Atomic load takes place. This process should take a fraction of a second.
8. The Queue is released and all of the packets are handled by the new policy.

> **Note:** Additional steps may be included for debugging purposes.

# *NAT*

Network Address Translation (NAT) and Network Address Port Translation (NAPT) are the two primary technologies traditionally used as methods to:

- Hide networks so that actual IP addresses are not revealed or required to be publicly routable. This reduces the need for more publicly routable IPs.
- Allow access to internal (sometimes, non-routable) resources from an external network.

## How NAT Works

When referring to NAT in the firewall context, it is not only meant in the traditional sense, but to regard NAT as an infrastructure of services used, for example, to create clustering solutions, security servers, office mode connections, etc.

| | |
|---|---|
| Infrastructure | • INSPECT rules and tables<br>• Performed on the first packet |
| Features | • NAT rule base is efficient<br>• Dual NAT (Automatic rules)<br>• Rule Priorities |

When NAT is defined on a network object, NAT rules are automatically added to the NAT Rule Base. Those are called Automatic NAT rules. NAT is translated during policy installation to tables and performed on the first packet of the connection. The NAT rule base is very efficient and can match two NAT rules on same connection; this is called bi-directional NAT and only applies for Automatic rules.

**Note:** Even though NAT merges two automatic NAT rules into one, as described above, this featured may be disabled and NAT rules may be manually defined for additional options.

NAT rules are prioritized first match manual/pre-automatic NAT rules, then automatic NAT rules (static NAT first, followed by Hide NAT) then post-automatic manual NAT rules..

## Hide NAT Process

Consider first the original packet. When the packet arrives at the inbound interface, it is inspected by the Security Policy. If accepted, the packet is entered into the connections table. The first packet of the connection is matched against NAT rules. The packet is translated if a match is found. Then the packet arrives at the TCP/IP stack of the Firewall Module machine, and is routed to the outbound interface.

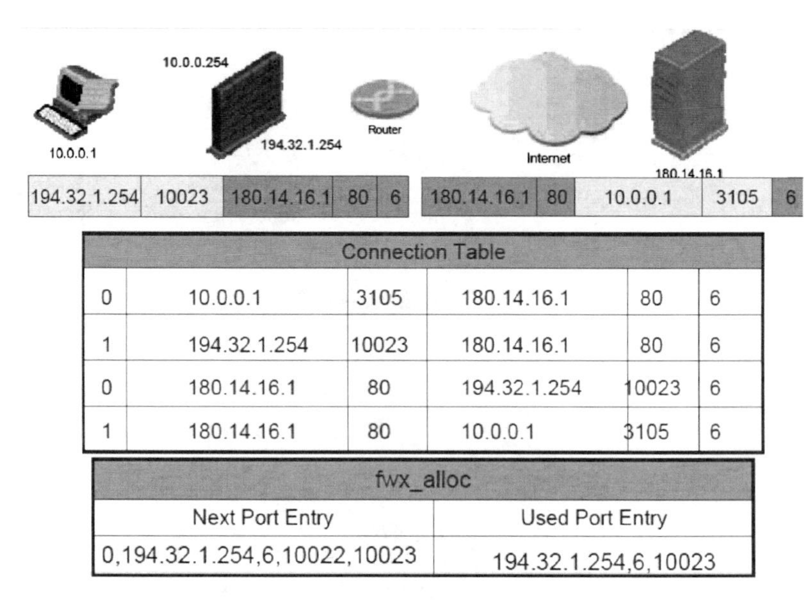


| Connection Table | | | | | |
|---|---|---|---|---|---|
| 0 | 10.0.0.1 | 3105 | 180.14.16.1 | 80 | 6 |
| 1 | 194.32.1.254 | 10023 | 180.14.16.1 | 80 | 6 |
| 0 | 180.14.16.1 | 80 | 194.32.1.254 | 10023 | 6 |
| 1 | 180.14.16.1 | 80 | 10.0.0.1 | 3105 | 6 |

| fwx_alloc | |
|---|---|
| Next Port Entry | Used Port Entry |
| 0,194.32.1.254,6,10022,10023 | 194.32.1.254,6,10023 |

Figure 16 — Hide NAT

During the NAT rule base traversal, both NAT source and destination are decided. However, they are actually performed at the appropriate locations:

- **src nat** on the server side
- **dst nat** depending on the relevant GUI property

The Reply packet arrives at the inbound interface of the firewall machine. The packet is passed by the Security Policy since it is found in the connections table. The packet's destination, which is the source of the original packet, is translated according to the NAT information. This takes place when the packet was translated in the first initial connection. The packet arrives at the TCP/IP stack of the firewall machine, and is routed to the outbound interface. The packet goes through the outbound interface, and its source, the destination of the original packet, is translated according to the information in the NAT tables. The packet leaves the firewall machine.

## Security Servers

Another important feature of the Check Point firewall, Security Servers are a necessary and crucial element to firewall functionality. Some firewall features require a higher layer protocol enforcement such as the application layer. In addition, authentication schemes such as User, Client and Session authentication requires that the firewall maintain the connection during the user session, so that processes must be maintained and monitored. To accomplish this, the firewall acts as a proxy (only for user authentication) and the user-mode processes are employed to manage this activity.

**Note:** When Identity Awareness is deployed, this process is operates differently.

## How a Security Server Works

Essentially, when a client initiates a connection to a server, the firewall kernel signals the FWD process using a trap. FWD spawns the FWSSD child service, which runs the security server. Then, the security server binds to a socket and manages the connection.

FWD waits for connections on the ports of other servers (daemons), and starts the corresponding server when the connection is made. FWD also talks to its children processes on other servers using a pipe and by using signals.

In the file structure, the real_port is the port being bound to. If 'real_port' is 0, a high random port will be assigned. The **$FWDIR/conf/fwauthd.conf** file structure is as follows:

**<logical_port> <server>**
**<real_port> <opt args>**

## Basic Firewall Administration

In addition to understanding the Firewall kernel structure, it is important to familiarize yourself about configuration file structure along with commands typically used for troubleshooting problems. To begin with, lets consider how the firewall configuration files are broken down. The main sub-grouping of configuration files are divided into directories located under **/opt**.

- **CPsuite-R76** — Manages firewall modules (R70 - R76). CPsuite is the generic installation.
- **CPshrd-R76** — Stores what used to be called SVN foundation including CPD database, licenses, registry and generic low level Check Point infrastructure. (not version related)
- **CPvsxngxcmp** — For managing VSX
- **CPedgecmp** — For managing Edge devices

In addition, the **/lib** and **/conf** directories store definitions files important to take into consideration. For instance, the **$FWDIR/lib/*.def** files include rulebase and protocol definitions. Users definitions are stored in **$FWDIR/conf/fwauth.NDB**, and security server configuration settings are stored in **$FWDIR/conf/fwauthd.conf**.

**$FWDIR/conf/classes.C** defines fields for each object used in the objects_5_0.C file, such as color, num/string, and default value. Though the **$FWDIR/database/** directory on the Management Server has no relevancy, this directory is particularly noteworthy on the gateway itself, where specific object entries are stored for that particular gateway. **$FWDIR/conf/** on the Management Server is also not relevant, but **$FWDIR/lib/*.def** is not important on the gateway.

There are two ways to view and edit database files such as these.

- **dbedit** — A command line utility on the Management server itself.
- **GUIdbedit.exe** — A executable tool located on the Windows-based GUI client machine under:
  **C:\Program Files\CheckPoint\SmartConsole\R75\Program**.

## Common Commands

Note the following commonly used commands in troubleshooting gateways:

- **cpconfig** — Used to run a command line version of the Check Point Configuration tool, and to configure or reconfigure a Security Gateway/ Management installation.
- **cplic print** — Located in **$CPDIR/bin**, this command prints details of Check Point licenses on the local machine. **Cplic print –x** prints the licenses with signatures and **cplic del <signature>** deletes a license.
- **cpstart** — This command is used to start all Check Point processes and applications running on a machine.
- **cpstop** — This command is used to terminate all Check Point processes and applications, running on a machine.

The commands **cpstop** and **cpstart** are actually calling **fwstop** and **fwstart** scripts for all Check Point product, including the firewall stop/start scripts located in **$FWDIR/bin**. These are scripts that actually run when you perform **cpstop**, **cpstart** and **cprestart** with different flags. **Cprestart** is an "internal" command used for DAIP (Dynamically Assigned IP devices) such as Edge devices. Not all CP processes are actually brought down when you use **cprestart**, so always use **cpstop** and **cpstart**, and not **cprestart**.

# *FW Monitor*

As an aid to understanding the Firewall "under-the-hood" and developing good debugging skills, the Check Point tool, FW Monitor is key and essential in packet capture and firewall traffic analysis.

**Note:** Check Point recommends turning off SecureXL (**fwaccel off**) when using **fw monitor**.

## What is FW Monitor?

FW Monitor is a packet analyzer tool available on every Check Point Security Gateway. It provides kernel level inspection but will not run in promiscuous mode. FW Monitor works for layers 3 and above in the OSI network layer stack. The syntax is the same regardless of the platform, and supports the.CAP output format used in Ethereal and Wireshark packet analyzer tools.

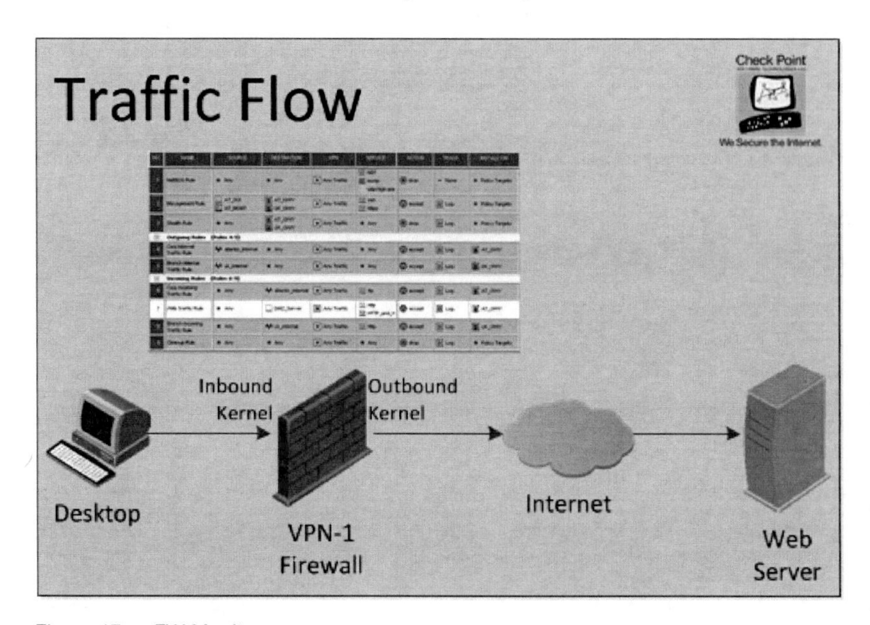


Figure 17 — FW Monitor

## C2S Connections and S2C Packets

FW Monitor captures packets as they enter and leave the firewall kernel and when the packet enters and leaves the inbound and outbound chains respectively. In the case of client to server communication, a client designated as Host1 according to the policy sends traffic destined for a Web server located behind the firewall. Since the traffic is permitted passage through the firewall based on the policy rulebase, the packet must traverse and be inspected by both chains of the firewall.

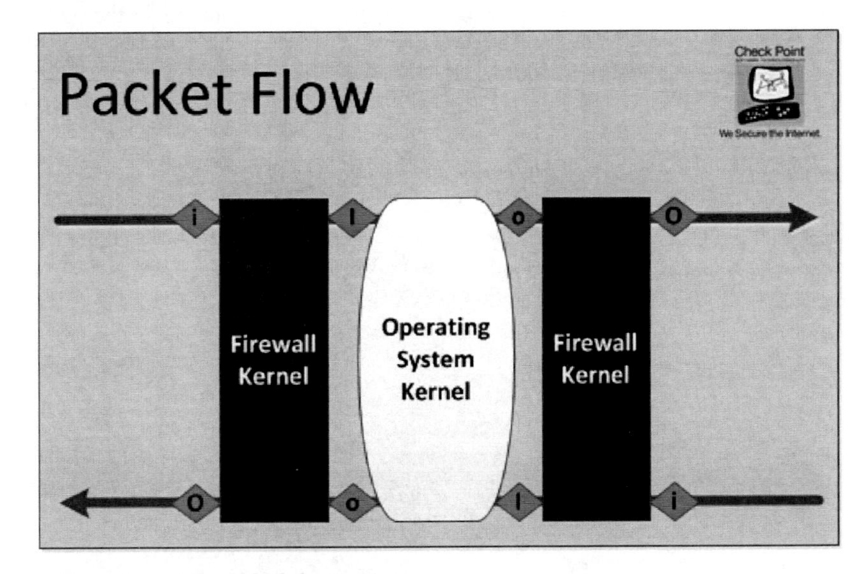


Figure 18 — 2S and S2C Connections

FW Monitor works by loading a special INSPECT filter to filter out interesting packets. This filter is different from the INSPECT filter used to implement a rule base. Where the rule base determines which packet is accepted, rejected, or dropped, the INSPECT filter generated by fw monitor simply captures kernel packet flows. You can capture everything through the kernel using fw monitor, even a particular type of traffic or source.

Once fw monitor is executed, the specified INSPECT filter is compiled and loaded to the kernel. Any parameters following "accept" in the fw monitor command will be displayed by fw monitor. The same filter is executed on all interfaces in all directions.

The fw monitor output uses specific expressions to explain the location of the packet as it moves through the firewall. There are four inspection points as a packet passes through the kernel (or virtual machine):

**i** — Before the virtual machine, in the inbound direction (pre-inbound)

**I** — After the virtual machine, in the inbound direction (post-inbound)

**o** — Before the virtual machine, in the outbound direction (pre-outbound)

**O** — After the virtual machine, in the outbound direction (post-outbound)

In our client to server scenario, 'i' represents the packet as it left the client. The 'I' represents the packet already checked against the tables and rule base. In case of Static NAT, the destination IP address will be changed. The 'o' means the packet is before the outbound kernel (same as 'I'), and 'O' means the packet is in the outbound kernel chain, as it will appear at the Web server. In the case of Hide NAT, the source IP address will be different here.

For packets traveling from server to client, the inspection points are just the reverse, where 'I' could be the NAT'ed packet on its way out of the inbound chain in the firewall in the case of Static NAT. At this point, the packet has already been checked by the tables and rule base. The 'O' is the packet as it will appear to the client.

## fw monitor

In a busy system, running fw monitor without any filters can create a great detail of output, and makes the analysis difficult. Filter expressions are available used to specify packets to be captured and limit the amount of output. The general syntax is:

```
fw monitor -e "accept <expression>;"
```

# Practice and Review

## Practice Lab

Lab 2: Core CLI Elements of Firewall Administration

## Review Questions

1. The core process CPD provides what main functions?

2. The firewall's kernel consists of two completely separate logical parts representing the process of a packet coming into and out from the firewall, these are referred to as...

CHAPTER 3

# *Clustering and Acceleration*

# *Clustering and Acceleration*

Whether your preferred network redundancy protocol is Check Point ClusterXL technology or standard VRRP protocol, it is no longer a "platform choice" you will have to make with Gaia. Both ClusterXL and VRRP are fully supported by Gaia, and Gaia is available to all Check Point Appliances, open servers and virtualized environments. There are no more trade-off decisions between required network protocols and preferred security platforms/functions.

## Objectives

- Build, test and troubleshoot a ClusterXL Load Sharing deployment on an enterprise network.
- Build, test and troubleshoot a ClusterXL High Availability deployment on an enterprise network.
- Build, test and troubleshoot a management HA deployment on an enterprise network.
- Configure, maintain and troubleshoot SecureXL and CoreXL acceleration solutions on the corporate network traffic to ensure noted performance enhancement on the firewall.
- Build, test and troubleshoot a VRRP deployment on an enterprise network.

# VRRP

VRRP (Virtual Routing Redundancy Protocol) is a cluster solution where two or more Gaia-based Security Gateways work together as one Security Gateway. You can configure your VRRP cluster for high availability or load sharing.

The Virtual Router Redundancy Protocol (VRRP) eliminates the single point of failure, while maintaining a single router's ease of administration. VRRP enables additional routers to take over the role of a failed first hop router, helping them to avoid becoming the single point of failure for network services.

The Check Point implementation of VRRP includes additional functionality called Monitored Circuit VRRP. Monitored-Circuit VRRP prevents "black holes" caused by asymmetric routes created when only one interface on master router fails (as opposed to the master itself). Gaia releases priority over all interfaces on a virtual router to let failover occur.

You cannot deploy a standalone deployment (Security Gateway and Security Management server on the same computer) in a Gaia VRRP cluster.

## VRRP vs ClusterXL

VRRP and ClusterXL are mutually exclusive, you can use either, but not both at the same time.

### *Advantages of using ClusterXL*

ClusterXL provides high availability and load sharing. It distributes traffic between clusters of redundant gateways so that the computing capacity of multiple machines may be combined to increase total throughput. If an individual gateway becomes unreachable, all connections are redirected to a designated backup without interruption. Tight integration with Check Point management and enforcement points ensures simple deployment.

- Transparent failover
- Higher performance
- Easy deployment
- Cost-effective

### *Advantages of using VRRP:*

- Minimizes failover time (Black Holes) and bandwidth overhead when a primary router becomes unavailable.

- VRRP supports up to 255 virtual routers (VRRP Groups) on a router physical interface, subject to the platform supporting multiple MAC addresses.
- Minimizes service disruptions during failover.
- Provides for election of multiple virtual routers on a network for load sharing.
- Addresses failover problems at the router level instead of on the network edge.
- Avoids the need to make configuration changes in the end nodes if a gateway router fails.
- Eliminates the need for router discovery protocols to support failover operations.
- Functions over a wide variety of multi-access LAN technologies capable of supporting IP traffic.

Illustrated is a simple VRRP configuration, where Platform A is the Master, and Platform B is the backup.

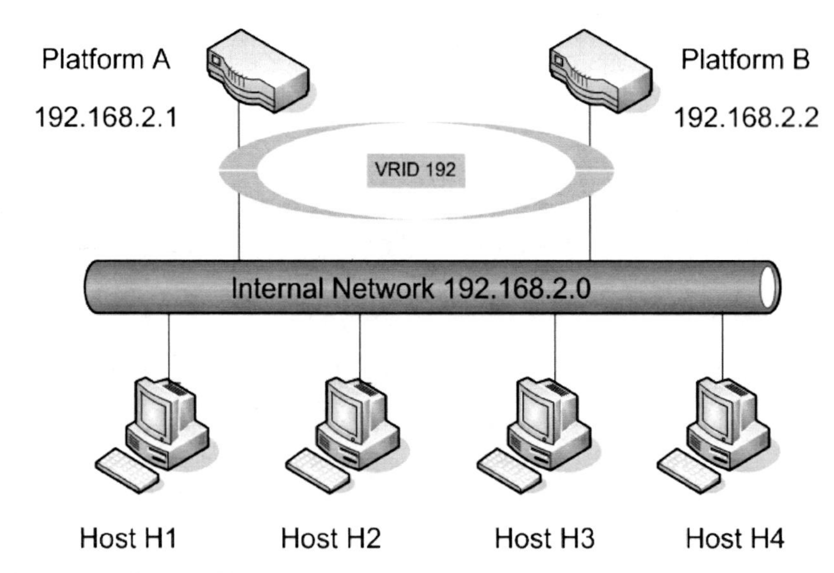


Figure 19 — Simple VRRP

A VRRP router (a router that is running VRRP) might participate in more than one VRID. The VRID mappings and priorities are different for each VRID. You can create two VRIDs on the master and backup platforms. One VRID for connections with the external network, and one for connection with the internal network.

This next diagram shows VRRP Configuration with Internal and External VRIDs.

In this example, Platform A acts as the master for VRID 1 and VRID 2, while Platform B acts as the backup for VRID 1 and VRID 2.

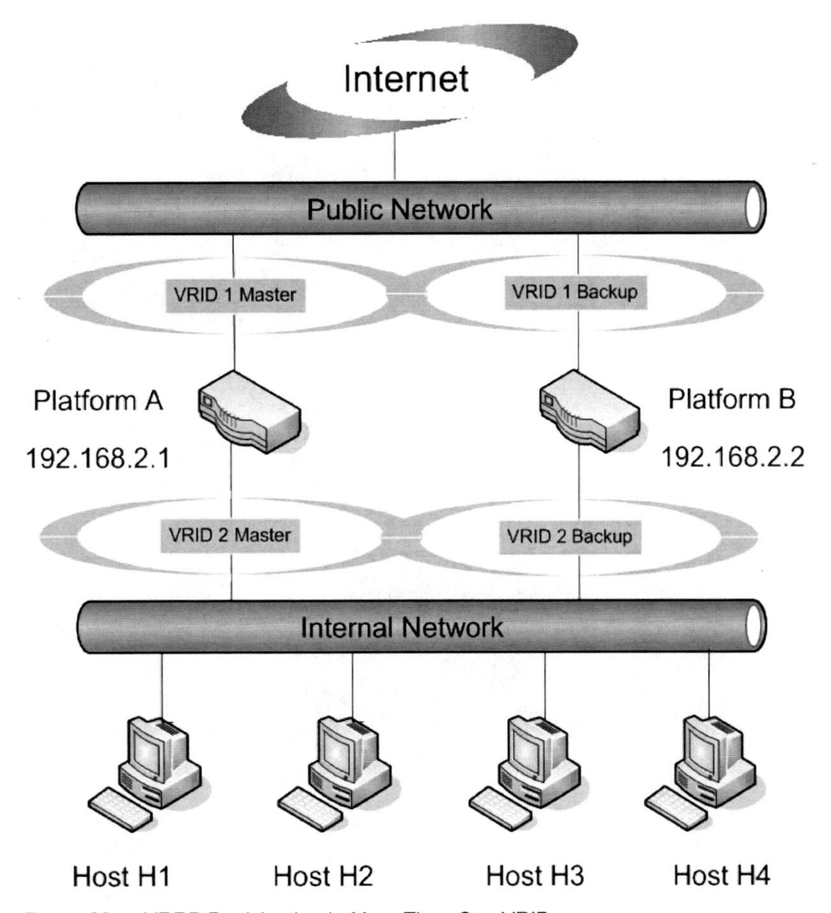


Figure 20 — VRRP Participation in More Than One VRID

You can configure some platforms to be part of multiple VRIDs while they simultaneously back up each other. This is known as an active-active configuration.

In this next active-active configuration, two VRIDs are implemented on the internal network for load sharing. Platform A is the master for VRID 5, and is the default gateway for Host H1 and Host H2. Platform B is the master for VRID 7, and is the default gateway for Host H3 and Host H4. Platforms A and B are configured to back each other up.

If one platform fails, the other takes its VRID and IP addresses. It supplies load balancing, full redundancy, and uninterrupted service to the default IP addresses.

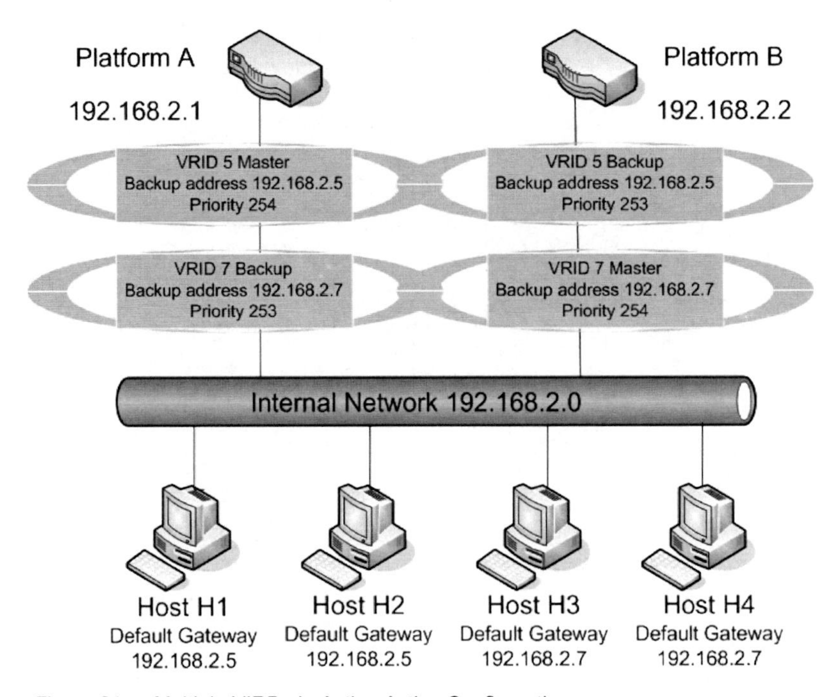


Figure 21 — Multiple VIRDs in Active-Active Configuration

### *VRRP Configurations*

You can configure VRRP using one of these procedures:

1. VRRP (Simple Monitored Circuit VRRP)

   The simple Monitored Circuit VRRP configuration contains all of the basic parameters and is applicable for most environments.

2. Advanced VRRP - use this procedure if you are working with:

   - A system on which VRRP has already been configured using this method.

   - An environment where it is necessary to monitor each interface individually.

   - You can change the VMAC (Virtual MAC Address) assignment mode.

The advanced VRRP requires users to manually configure a virtual router for each monitored interface

You cannot use the easy and advanced procedures to configure Monitored-Circuit VRRP on the same computer.

## Monitored Circuit VRRP

Monitored-circuit VRRP eliminates "black holes" caused by asymmetric routes that can be created if only one interface on the master fails (as opposed to the entire platform). Gaia does this by reducing priority over all of the interfaces in the virtual router to allow the backup to take over entirely.

If you are using standard VRRPv2 and the external interface fails or becomes unreachable, the external virtual router fails over to the backup while the internal virtual router stays on the master. This can result in reachability failures, as the platform might accept packets from an internal end host but be unable to forward them to destinations that are reached through the failed interface to the external network.

Monitored-circuit VRRP monitors all of the VRRP-configured interfaces on the platform. If an interface fails, the master releases its priority over all of the VRRP-configured interfaces. This allows the backup platform to take over all of the interfaces and become master for both the internal and external VRID.

To release the priority, Gaia subtracts the priority delta, a Check Point-specific parameter that you configure when you set up the VRID, from the priority to calculate an effective priority. If you configure your system correctly, the effective priority is lower than that of the backup routers and, therefore, the VRRP election protocol is triggered to select a new master.

## Troubleshooting VRRP

You can log information about errors and events for troubleshooting VRRP by enabling traces for VRRP.

To enable traces for VRRP:

1. In the WebUI tree, select Routing > Routing Options.
2. In the Trace Options section, in the Filter Visible Tables Below drop down list, select VRRP.
3. In the VRRP table, select an option, and click Activate.

The system restarts the routing subsystem and signals it to reread its configuration. The option you selected, its name and On/Off radio buttons show on the page.

If VRRP failover does not occur as expected, make sure of the configuration of these items.

- All routers of a VRRP group must have the same system times. The simplest method to synchronize times is to enable NTP on all nodes of the VRRP group. You can also manually change the time and time zone on each node to match the other nodes. It must be no more than seconds apart.

- All routers of a VRRP group must have the same Hello Interval.
- The Priority Delta must be sufficiently large for the Effective Priority to be lower than the backup router. Otherwise, when you pull an interface for a Monitored-Circuit VRRP test, other interfaces do not release IP addresses.
- You can use different encryption accelerator cards in two appliances of one VRRP group or IP cluster (such as the Check Point Encrypt Card in one appliance, and the older Check Point Encryption Accelerator Card in a different appliance). When you do, select encryption/authentication algorithms supported on the two cards. If the encryption/authentication algorithm is supported on the master only, and you use NAT, tunnels failover incorrectly. If the encryption/authentication algorithm is supported on the master only, without NAT, tunnels are not accelerated after failover.
- VRIDs must be the same on all routers in a VRRP group. If you use Monitored-Circuit VRRP, make sure all platforms of one virtual IP address use the same VRID.
- The VRRP monitor in the WebUI might show one of the interfaces in initialize state. This might suggest that the IP address used as the backup address on that interface is invalid or reserved.
- SNMP Get on Interfaces might list the incorrect IP addresses. This results in incorrect Policy. An SNMP Get (for the Firewall object Interfaces in the GUI Security Policy editor) fetches the lowest IP address for each interface. If interfaces are created when the node is the VRRP master, the incorrect IP address might be included. To repair this problem, edit the interfaces by hand if necessary.

### *Firewall Policies*

If your platforms run firewall software, you must configure the firewall policies to accept VRRP packets. The multicast destination assigned by the IANA for VRRP is 224.0.0.18. If the policy does not accept packets to 224.0.0.18, firewall platforms in the same VRRP group take on Master state.

### *Monitored-Circuit VRRP in Switched Environments*

With Monitored-Circuit VRRP, some Ethernet switches might not recognize the VRRP MAC address after a master to backup change. This is because many switches cache the MAC address related to the Ethernet device attached to a port. When the change to a backup router occurs, the MAC address for virtual router shifts to a different port. Switches that cache the MAC address might not change to the correct port during a VRRP change.

To repair this problem, you can take one of the these actions:

- Replace the switch with a hub.
- Disable MAC address caching on the switch, or switch ports that the security platforms are connected to.

It might be not possible to disable the MAC address caching. If so, set the address aging value sufficiently low that the addresses age out each second or two. This causes more overhead on the switch. Therefore, find out if this is a viable option for the model of switch you run.

The Spanning Tree protocol prevents Layer 2 loops across multiple bridges. Spanning-Tree can be enabled on the ports connected to the two sides of a VRRP pair. It can also see multicast Hello Packets come for the same MAC address from two different ports. When the two occur, it can suggest a loop, and the switch blocks traffic from one port. If a port is blocked, no security platforms in the VRRP pair can get Hello Packets from the other. In this instance, the two of them enter the master router state.

Enable PortFast on the ports connected to the VRRP pair. PortFast causes a port to enter the Spanning-Tree forwarding state immediately, by passing the listening and learning states. The command to enable PortFast is set spantree portfast 3/1-2 enable, where 3/1-2 refers to slot 3, ports 1 and 2.

# Clustering and Acceleration

The Check Point Acceleration and Clustering Software Blade grants two features - load-sharing modes of ClusterXL (unicast/pivot and multicast), and SecureXL that work together to maximize performance and security in high-performance environments. These work with CoreXL, which is included with the software blade containers, to form the foundation of the Open Performance Architecture, which delivers throughput designed for data center applications and the high levels of security needed to protect against today's application-level threats.

**Note:** The Acceleration and Clustering Software Blade is NOT required for ClusterXL HA and VRRP.

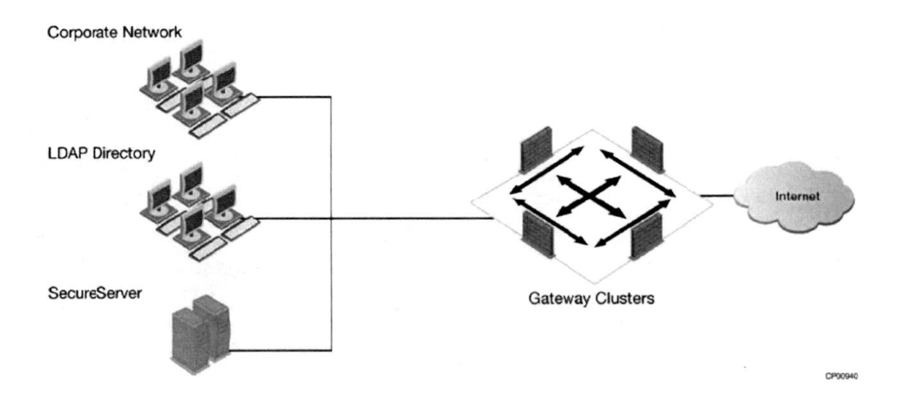


Figure 22 — Clustering

## Clustering Terms

Check Point uses the following terms when discussing clustering:

- **Active Up** —When the High Availability machine that was Active and suffered a failure becomes available again, it returns to the cluster, not as the Active machine but as one of the standby machines in the cluster.
- **Critical Device** — A device that the Administrator has defined to be critical to the operation of the cluster member. A critical device is also known as a Problem Notification (pnote). Critical devices are constantly monitored. If a critical device stops functioning, this is defined as a failure. A device can be hardware or a process. The **`fwd`** and **`cphad`** processes, as well as the Security Policy itself are predefined by default as critical devices. The Administrator can add to the list of critical devices using the **`cphaprob`** command.
- **Failure** — A hardware or software problem that causes a machine to be unable to filter packets. A failure of an Active machine leads to a Failover.
- **Failover** — A machine taking over packet filtering in place of another machine in the cluster that suffered a failure.
- **High Availability (HA)** — The ability to maintain a connection when there is a failure by having another machine in the cluster take over the connection, without any loss of connectivity. As opposed to Load Sharing, in this case, only the Active machine filters packets. One of the machines in the cluster is configured as the Active machine. If a failure occurs on the Active machine, one of the other machines in the cluster assumes its responsibilities
- **Hot Standby** — Also known as *Active/Standby.* It has the same meaning as **High Availability**.
- **Cluster Control Protocol** — Cluster Control Protocol or CCP is used specifically for Clustered environments to allow for gateways to report their own states and learn about the states of other members in the cluster. It is the essential means by which State Synchronization works, in order to provide failover in the event an active member goes down.

There is no need to add a rule to the Rule Base that accepts CCP. When clustering is configured on the gateways, an implied rule is created making this provision.

State Synchronization traffic typically makes up around 90 percent of all Cluster Control Protocol (CCP) traffic. State Synchronization packets are distinguished from the rest of CCP traffic via an opcode in the UDP data header.

## ClusterXL

As a network and security professional, you are often required to consider the needs of an organization and weigh them against available resources, to provide the most cost effective solution. Often this requires addressing risk management without significantly increasing cost. A direct result from risk assessments is often the concern for hardware backups and resource utilization due to increasing network traffic. To address this, we will look at the clustering and acceleration solutions provided by Check Point, how they should be implemented into the working network, and how to troubleshoot issues whenever they occur.

Ensuring that Security Gateways and VPN connections are kept alive in a corporate network is critical to maintain "business as usual". The failure of a Security Gateway or VPN connection can result in the loss of active connections and access to critical data. As a network security expert, it is your job to maintain the dependability of these business-critical devices.

ClusterXL supplies an infrastructure that ensures that no data is lost in case of a system failure. Essentially, a cluster is a group of identical security gateways connected in such a way that if one fails, another immediately takes its place. Check Point ClusterXL provides both Load Sharing as well as High Availability solutions.

- High Availability ensures gateway and VPN redundancy for transparent failover between machines.
- Load Sharing provides reliability and enhances performance because all cluster members are active.

ClusterXL must be installed in a distributed configuration in which the Security Management server and the cluster members are on different machines. ClusterXL is part of the standard Security Gateway installation.

Both the plug-and-play and the evaluation licenses include the option to work with up to three ClusterXL Load Sharing clusters managed by the same Security Management server.

ClusterXL supported platforms are listed in the platform support matrix, which is available online at:

`http://support.checkpoint.com`

ClusterXL uses unique physical IP and MAC addresses for the cluster members and virtual IP addresses to represent the cluster itself. Virtual IP addresses do not belong to an actual machine interface.

When using ClusterXL, ensure that you synchronize the clocks of all of the cluster members. You can synchronize the clocks manually or using NTP. Features such as VPN function properly only once the clocks of all of the cluster members are synchronized.

## Cluster Synchronization

In order to make sure each gateway cluster member is aware of the connections going through the other members, a mechanism called State Synchronization exists which allows status information about connections on the Security Gateways to be shared between the members.

State Synchronization enables all machines in the cluster to be aware of the connections passing through each of the other machines. It ensures that if there is a failure in a cluster member, connections that were handled by the failed machine will be maintained by the other machines.

Every IP based service, including TCP and UDP, recognized by the Security Gateway is synchronized.

State Synchronization is used both by ClusterXL and by third-party OPSEC-certified clustering products.

State Synchronization works in two modes:

- **Full synchronization** — transfers all firewall kernel table information from one cluster member to another. It is handled by the **`fwd`** daemon, using an encrypted TCP connection.
- **Delta synchronization** — transfers changes in the kernel tables between cluster members. Delta sync is handled by the firewall kernel, using UDP multicast or broadcast on port 8116.

Full synchronization is used for initial transfers of state information, for many thousands of connections. If a cluster member is brought up after failing down, it will perform full sync. Once all members are synchronized, only updates are transferred via delta sync. Delta sync is much quicker than full sync.

Running **cphastart** on a cluster member activates ClusterXL on the member. It does not initiate full synchronization. cpstart is the recommended way to start a cluster member. Running cphastop on a cluster member stops the cluster member from passing traffic. State synchronization also stops. It is still possible to open connections directly to the cluster member. These commands should only be run by the Security Gateway, and not directly by the user.

## Synchronized-Cluster Restrictions

The following restrictions apply to synchronizing cluster members:

- Only cluster members running on the same platform can be synchronized.
- The cluster members must be of the same software version.
- A User Authenticated connection through a cluster member will be lost if the cluster member fails. Other synchronized cluster members will be unable to resume the connection. However, a Client Authenticated or Session Authenticated connection will not be lost.

  The User Authentication state is maintained on Security Servers, which are processes, and thus cannot be synchronized on different machines in the way that kernel data can be synchronized. However, the state of Session Authentication and Client Authentication is stored in kernel tables, and so can be synchronized.
- The state of connections using resources is maintained in a Security Server, so these connections cannot be synchronized for the same reason that User Authenticated connections cannot be synchronized.
- Accounting information is accumulated in each cluster member and reported separately to the Security Management Server, where the information is aggregated. In case of a failover, accounting information that was accumulated on the failed member but not yet reported to the Security Management Server is lost. To minimize the problem, it is possible to reduce the period in which accounting information is flushed. To do this, in the cluster object's **Logs and Masters** > **Additional Logging** window, configure the attribute **Update Account Log every**.

## Securing the Sync Interface

Since the synchronization network carries the most sensitive Security Policy information in the organization, it is critical to protect it against both malicious and unintentional threats. Check Point recommends securing the synchronization interfaces either by:

- Using a dedicated sync network
- Connecting the physical network interfaces of the cluster members directly using a cross-over cable. In a cluster having three or more members, us a hub or switch.

## To Synchronize or Not to Synchronize

In general, all connections on a cluster are synchronized between members, with a few exceptions. You may choose not to synchronize certain types of connections, either because:

- A significant load on the network is caused by the use of a particular service.
- A service may open many short connections, whose loss may not be very important, or even noticed, i.e., DNS (over UDP), HTTP.
- Bi-directional stickiness (to be discussed later in this chapter) is employed for all connections, i.e., LS mode with no VPN or static NAT, some OPSEC clusters.

For all TCP services whose protocol type is HTTP or None, you can configure the Security Gateway to delay a connection so that it will only be synchronized if it still exists after the connection is initiated for *x* seconds. This capability is only available if a SecureXL-enabled devices is installed on the gateway to which the packet passes. (SecureXL will be covered later in this chapter.)

# *ClusterXL: Load Sharing*

In a Load Sharing Gateway Cluster, all cluster members are active, so it brings significant performance advantages. Using multiple gateways instead of a single gateway increases linear performance for CPU intensive applications such as VPNs, Security servers, Policy servers, and User Directory (LDAP).

There are two available modes which work in a Load Sharing deployment:

- Multicast
- Unicast

Machines in a ClusterXL Load Sharing configuration must be synchronized. Machines in a ClusterXL High Availability configuration do not have to be synchronized, but connections will be lost upon failover if they are not.

## Multicast Load Sharing

In ClusterXL's Load Sharing Multicast mode, every member of the cluster receives all of the packets sent to the cluster IP address. When a router or Layer 3 switch forwards packets to all of the cluster members using multicast, a ClusterXL decision algorithm on all cluster members decides which cluster member should perform enforcement processing on the packet. Only that machine processes the packet, and sends the packet to its destination; the other machines drop the packet.

Only routers or layer 3 switches that accept a multicast MAC address as a response to an ARP request with a unicast IP address are supported for multicast load sharing.

## Unicast Load Sharing

In ClusterXL's Load Sharing Unicast mode, one machine, called the **Pivot**, receives all traffic from a router with a unicast configuration and redistributes the packets to the other machines in the cluster. The Pivot machine is chosen automatically by ClusterXL.

The Pivot is the only machine that communicates with the router. In this scheme, the router uses only the Pivot's unicast MAC address to communicate to the cluster.

The Pivot functions as a cluster router, both from the internal network outwards, and vice versa. This functionality also applies to DMZ networks.

After the Pivot first receives the packet from the router or switch, the Pivot's Load Sharing decision function decides which cluster member should handle the packet. This decision function is made in a similar fashion to the regular multicast Load Sharing decision. The Pivot may also decide to handle the packet itself. In such a case, Pivot Load Sharing will hand the packet to the Pivot's Firewall component for processing.

Because the Pivot is busy distributing traffic, the Pivot participates to a lesser extent in the actual load sharing function. The other cluster members take on more traffic load. Since the Check Point Pivot Mode feature is based on unicast addresses only, it can work with all routers and Layer 3 switches.

## How Packets Travel Through a Unicast LS Cluster

When the router first sends a packet through the cluster, the following occurs:

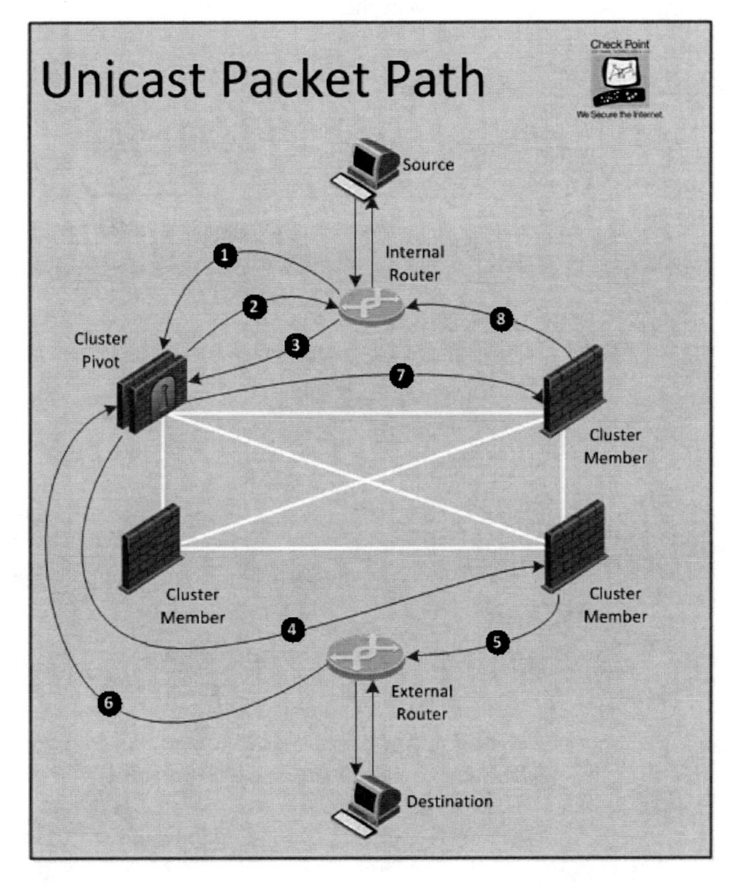


Figure 23 — Unicast Packet Path

1. The router sends an ARP request for the cluster IP address.
2. The Pivot returns an ARP reply, with its own unicast MAC address, to the router.
3. The router sends the packet to the Pivot.
4. The Pivot forwards the packet to the designated cluster member, without changing the packet. The destination IP address of the packet remains unchanged, and neither decryption nor NAT functionality is performed on the forwarded packet. When sending the packet, the Pivot uses the MAC address of the designated cluster member. The packet is forwarded through the original interface.
5. The cluster member that receives the forwarded packet performs the inspection, and sends the packet to its destination.

   The return packet goes through the same process, although it may not necessarily be forwarded by the Pivot to the same cluster member. The process of the return packet is as follows:

   a. The return packet first reaches the Pivot, which assigns the cluster member to handle the packet.

   b. The packet is forwarded to the cluster member for Security Gateway inspection.

   c. The cluster member sends the packet to its destination.

## Sticky Connections

A connection is sticky when all of its packets are handled, in either direction, by a single cluster member. This is the case in High Availability mode, where all connections are routed through the same cluster member.

In Load Sharing mode, there are cases where it is necessary to ensure that a connection that starts on a specific cluster member will continue to be processed by the same cluster member in both directions. To that end, certain connections can be made sticky by enabling the Sticky Decision Function.

### *The Sticky Decision Function*

The Sticky Decision Function enables certain services to operate in a Load Sharing deployment. For example, it is required for L2TP traffic, or when the cluster is a participant in a site-to-site VPN tunnel with a third-party peer.

The following services and connection types are supported by enabling the Sticky Decision Function:

- VPN deployments with third-party VPN peers
- Endpoint Connect/SSL Network Extender encrypted connections

The Sticky Decision Function is not supported when employing either Performance Pack or a hardware-based accelerator card. Enabling the Sticky Decision Function disables these acceleration products.

When the Sticky Decision Function is used, cluster members are prevented from opening more than one connection to a specific peer. Opening another connection would cause another SA to be generated, which a third-party peer would not be able to process in many cases.

# Maintenance Tasks and Tools

The following covers topics relevant to an administrators' everyday maintenance of a clustered environment.

## Perform a Manual Failover of the FW Cluster

The best practice method for initiating a failover administratively in a controlled manner (not failure testing) is to run the following command on an active cluster member:

```
cphaprob -d STOP -s problem -t 0 register
```

The command actually creates a problem notification entry, with no refresh time, in a problem state. This will put the current machine into a problematic state. Running the command **cphaprob list** on this machine will show an entry named **STOP**.

To remove the problematic "STOP" entry from the cluster member, run the following command:

```
cphaprob -d STOP unregister
```

The above is a way of quickly and efficiently generating a gratuitous ARP from the cluster.

Another way is via the command:

```
$FWDIR/bin/clusterXL_admin <up|down>
```

Performing this command (**$FWDIR/bin/clusterXL_admin down**) on an active cluster member will initiate a failover to the standby cluster member. Make sure to perform **$FWDIR/bin/clusterXL_admin up** to normalize the environment.

> **Note:** A manual failover can also be induced from the Gateways Status screen in SmartView Monitor via "Stop Cluster Member...".

## Advanced Cluster Configuration Examples

*Example 1 - Setting CCP to use Broadcast*

The ClusterXL Control Protocol (CCP) on the cluster members uses multicast by default, because it is more efficient than broadcast. If the connecting switch is incapable of forwarding multicast traffic, it is possible, to change the CCP mode to broadcast. To change the CCP mode to broadcast, run the following command:

```
cphaconf set_ccp broadcast
```

To change back to multicast run the following command:

```
cphaconf set_ccp multicast
```

This traffic will be on UDP Port 8116.

This will survive a reboot. But as a precaution, the command needs to be added to `/etc/rc.local` file.

For verification, the command '`cphaprob -a if`' can be executed.

For Verizon Wireless, ClusterXL CCP must be set to BROADCAST mode.

*Example 2 - Multicast MAC Addresses*

To find out the multicast MAC address of a cluster, run command `cphaconf debug_data` on the Security Gateway.

The output of this command is written to `/var/log/messages` under the **Multicast table** section on each cluster member.

# Management HA

The Security Management server consists of several databases with information on different aspects of the system, such as objects, users and policy information. This data changes each time the system administrator makes modifications to the system. It is important to maintain a backup for this data, so that crucial information is not permanently lost in the event of Security Management Server failure.

Moreover, if the Security Management server fails or is down for administrative purposes, a backup server needs to be in place in order to take over its activities. In the absence of the Security Management Server, essential operations performed by the gateways, such as the fetching of the Security Policy and the retrieval of the CRL, cannot take place.

In Management HA, the Active Security Management server (Active SMS) always has one or more backup Standby Security Management servers (Standby SMS) which are ready to take over from the Active SMS. These SMS must all be of the same Operating System and version. The existence of the Standby SMS allows for crucial backups to be in place:

In a Management HA deployment, the first installed SMS is specified as the Primary Security Management server. This is a regular SMS used by the system administrator to manage the Security Policy. When any subsequent SMS is installed, these must be specified as Secondary SMS. Once the Secondary SMS has been installed and manually synchronized, the distinctions between Primary versus Secondary is no longer significant since either SMS an function as the Active SMS.

## The Management High Availability Environment

The Secondary SMS is created with empty databases. These databases are filled with information that the newly created Secondary SMS receives from the Active SMS. The Secondary SMS is ready once:

- It is represented on the Primary SMS by a network object.
- SIC has been initialized between it and the Primary SMS.
- Manual synchronization has been completed with the Primary SMS for the first time.

## Active vs. Standby

All management operations such as editing and installing the Security Policy and modifying users and objects, are done by the Active SMS. If the Active SMS is down, and any of these operations need to be performed, one of the Standby SMSs should be made active by the System Administrator. This transition from Standby to Active must be initiated manually.

The Standby SMSs are synchronized to the Active SMS, and therefore, are kept up-to-date with all changes in the databases and Security Policy. Security Gateways can fetch the Security Policy and retrieve a CRL from both the Active SMS and the Standby SMS.

## What Data is Backed Up?

In order for Management High Availability to function properly, there must be a backup of configuration and ICA data, such as:

- Databases (such as the Objects and Users)
- Certificate information such as Certificate Authority data and the CRL which is available to be fetched by the Check Point Security Gateways
- The installed Security Policy. The installed Security Policy is the applied Security Policy. The Security Gateways must be able to fetch the latest Security Policy from either the Active or the Standby SMS.

## Synchronization Modes

There are two ways to perform synchronization:

- Manual synchronization is a process initialized by the System Administrator. It can be set to synchronize databases, or databases as well as the installed Security Policy
- Automatic synchronization is configured by the System Administrator to allow the Standby SMSs to be synchronized with the Active SMSs at set intervals. This is the standard mode of synchronization, since it keeps the Standby SMSs updated. The synchronization schedule is based on when the Security Policy is installed; both the installed Security Policy and all the databases are synchronized. Additionally, it is possible to synchronize the Standby SMSs when the System Administrator saves the Security Policy or at a specified scheduled time.

It always possible to synchronize manually, even when automatic synchronization has been selected configured.

## Synchronization Status

The synchronization status indicates the status of the peer SMSs in relation to that of the selected SMS. This status can be viewed in the **Management High Availability Servers** window or in SmartView Monitor, depending on whether you are connected to the Active or Standby SMS.

- **Never been synchronized** — immediately after the Secondary Security Management server has been installed, it has not yet undergone the first manual synchronization that brings it up-to-date with the Primary Security Management server.
- **Synchronized** — the peer is properly synchronized and has the same database information and installed Security Policy
- **Lagging** — the peer SMS has not been synchronized since the Active SMS had changes applied to it.
- **Advanced** — the peer SMS is more up-to-date.
- **Collision** — the Active SMS and its peer have different installed policies and/or databases. The administrator must perform manual synchronization and decide which of the SMSs to overwrite. For example, when SMS A fails before a synchronization takes place, the changes made (to databases or to the Security Policy) cannot be synchronized with SMS B. When SMS B takes over from SMS A, the system administrator may decide to modify the Security Policy.

# *SecureXL: Security Acceleration*

Patented SecureXL is a technology interface that accelerates multiple, intensive security operations, including operations that are carried out by Check Point's Stateful Inspection firewall. Using SecureXL, the firewall offloads operations to a performance-optimized software or hardware device, dramatically increasing throughput

## What SecureXL Does

SecureXL accelerates firewall and VPN performance by remembering certain attributes of packets and packet flows that have already been validated by the firewall/VPN application. Then, validation of related packets and connections is delegated to the SecureXL API. This validation is done at the hardware interrupt level on x86 hardware, or supervises execution of further optimized code in attached network processors in IP security appliances that support them. Both of these approaches involve substantially less computing overhead than is required by the firewall/VPN application itself.

## Packet Acceleration

Packets attempting to establish a new TCP connection, or a comparable UDP connection table entry in the firewall, are handled in the "slowpath". Once the first packet is seen by the firewall and suitable connections/flows information is off-loaded to an appliance OS, for example, further packets are handled at the OS's interrupt-level code.

The round-trip processing-interrupt driver to application and back to driver-level code, is very time consuming, compared to the minimal processing necessary for later packets that can be done entirely at the driver level. Those later packets, determined to be part of an existing, already validated flow, are forwarded directly from the driver level without the added overhead of firewall application involvement.

SecureXL improved non-encrypted firewall traffic throughput, and encrypted VPN traffic throughput, by nearly an order-of-magnitude particularly for small packets flowing in long duration connections.

Packet acceleration is also referred to as **throughput acceleration** as it matches on the familiar 5-tuple of source address, destination address, source port, destination port, and protocol. However, only packets during the specific TCP/UDP connection can be accelerated.

## Session Rate Acceleration

SecureXL also reduces the overhead in establishing certain kinds of new connections, improving new connection rate (connections per second) and connection setup/teardown rate (sessions per second), as well as throughput in certain high-connection-rate traffic environments.

The principle involved is a simple extension of SecureXL's approach to “one-time validation” of a firewall flow. The one-time validation is extended from a particular 5-tuple - source address, destination address, source port, destination port, and protocol (one classic definition of a flow, or the definition of a microflow by Internet researchers) - to a range, or block, of one or more of these “tuples”.

Specifically, the source port of a flow may be masked off, effectively providing a global match for source port. That is, once a flow is validated and established, a template of that flow, with source port masked off, creating a global match, is saved and remembered (with a configurable time-out). Any new connection setup that matches four of the 5-tuples is again handled in the slowpath and not at the driver level. All the new connection creation/old connection deletion is handled in the slowpath. However, these new connection setup packets matching 4 out of 5 tuples avoid a round trip to the firewall application, and limit the computing overhead. Security is not impacted because the OS continues to track the state of the new connection using stateful inspection.

## Masking the Source Port

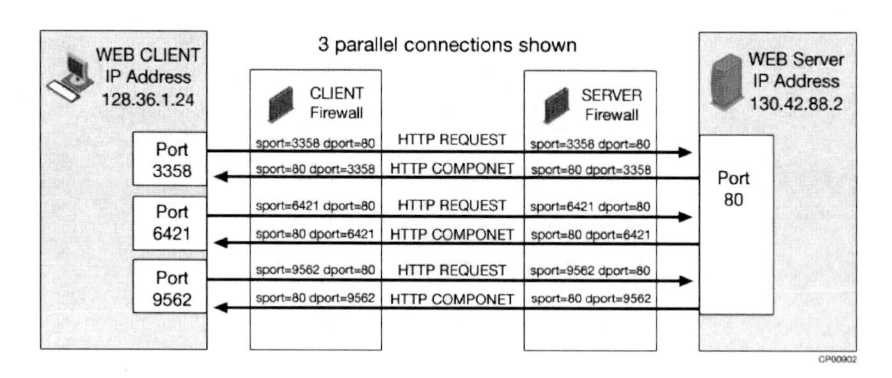


Figure 24 — Port Connections

To examine how ports are used in establishing TCP connections, consider the following scenario:

A client requesting a connection to a server will initiate the TCP three-way handshake. The client addresses the server, typically at a well-known port number depending on the service provided by the server (e.g. port 23 for Telnet, port 80 for HTTP). Together, the server's IP address and the well-known port number form a socket address. The client assigns and pairs an operating system selected port number with the client's IP address to create a socket address for the reverse direction.

## Application Layer Protocol - An example with HTTP

Consider higher-level application protocols that involve numerous TCP connections between the client and server - either simultaneously (in parallel) sequentially, or both. One of these protocols, which accounts for most Internet traffic, is HTTP.

Web pages consist of multiple HTTP components; text and perhaps dozens of graphic elements. Using HTTP 1.0, each component is downloaded from server to client using a separate TCP connection. This action involves substantial overhead in connection setup and tear-down, and further overhead in protective-firewall connection tracking (firewalls at both ends).

In all cases between a Web Client and a Web Server, TCP connection establishment is initiated by the Web Client, which then sends an HTTP request. The Web server responds by sending the HTTP component:

- HTTP Request (->) - Each of the packets from the Web client that requests an HTTP component from the Web Server has the same source address, destination address, destination port (80), and protocol (HTTP). Only the source port, assigned by the Web client's operation system, one per connection, differs in order to create unique socket addresses at the Client for each HTTP request/component (via separate TCP connections for each component).
- HTTP Component (<-) - Going the other direction, each of the packets from the Web server that build the Web page components on the Web client has the same source address, destination address, source port (80), and protocol (HTTP). Only the destination port differs (it's been assigned by the client operating system to that connection).

Let's look at applying SecureXL at the server Firewall. Once a connection involving a flow to port 80 is approved by the firewall application for the Web client (resulting from the first HTTP request) a template is created and stored. All subsequent connection setups carrying those additional requests can share that same template "approval" because its okay that the source ports differ. Establishing those subsequent connections does not involve a round trip to the firewall, resulting in faster processing through the server firewall.

Similarly, at the client Firewall, once a connection involving a flow to port 80 is approved by the firewall application (as above), all subsequent connections carrying these additional requests can share that same "approval." Establishing those subsequent connections does not involve a round-trip to the firewall. SecureXL accelerates subsequent connection establishment through both firewalls when multiple connections share the same source address, destination address, destination (server) port and protocol.

## HTTP 1.1

HTTP version 1.0 operates as described above, and SecureXL increases the connection establishment rate of the firewall for tracking these connections. This is because HTTP 1.0 creates a separate connection for each HTTP component. The newer HTTP version 1.1 improves the protocol's performance by permitting not only parallel, but also persistent and pipelined server connections. The server may keep the connection alive after sending the end of a component, which avoids the need to create a new connection to send the next component. HTTP 1.1 is supported by most Web servers and the current generation of browsers as well.

High connection-rate network environments involve primarily HTTP traffic. While HTTP 1.1 is significantly less connection-intensive, HTTP likely remains the protocol that generates most of the new connection requests in enterprise and Internet traffic. At the same time, while overall traffic levels continue to grow, connection rates grow less quickly as network environments use primarily HTTP 1.1.

SecureXL connection templates create the opportunity to generate extremely impressive connection rate performance. Given the benefit of connection templates in heavy HTTP environments, the significant performance increase can, in fact, be reflected in real-world traffic environments, particularly Web server farms and in enterprises where there is a great deal of Web traffic to a small, concentrated set of servers.

Other layer protocols such as UDP create many short lived connections in an HTTP page transfer, or extended streaming information can all be accelerated on a session basis and can greatly reduce resource overhead on a busy firewall. FTP and many types of VOIP have handlers which preclude acceleration.

## Factors that Preclude Acceleration

There are several factors that preclude a packet from being accelerated:

- SDF (Sticky Decision Function)
- QoS
- Connection destined to, or originated from the module
- Connections that require Security Servers (AUTH, AV, URLF, AS)
- Connections that have a Handler:
  ICMP, FTP, H323, etc
- Some IPS features
- IP ID, TTL, DNS Protocol enforcement
- Multicast packets

## Factors that Preclude Templating (Session Acceleration)

There are factors that can preclude templating, if all other parameters are met for packet acceleration.

- Time objects
- Dynamic objects
- Domain objects
- Source port ranges
- IPS features which are not supported in Acceleration
- NAT
- Encrypted Connections

Once templating is disabled in the rulebase, all connections matching rules lower in the rulebase cannot be templated. Use **`fwaccel stat`** to determine at which rule tempating is disabled and move the most used rules above that rule to take advantage of session acceleration.

## Packet Flow

The figure shows the decision logic for packets flowing through an SecureXL accelerated IP Security Appliances.

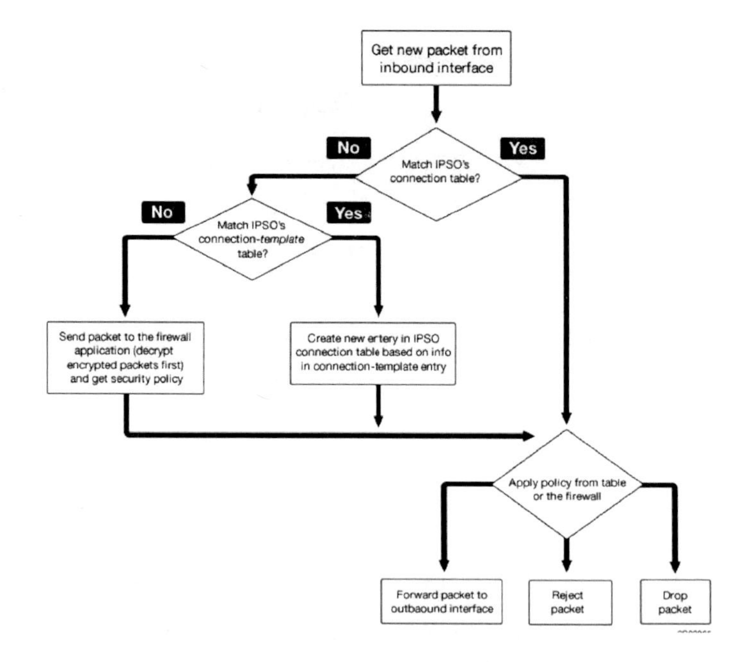


Figure 25 — Packet Flow Decision Logic

A new packet arrives at the inbound interface. The packet is checked against IPSO's connection table, which mirrors the Security Gateway's connection table. If there is a 5-tuple match (src, dst, sport, dport, proto), then the new packet is part of an existing flow and is forwarded to the outbound interface for handling (forward, drop, or reject). This path involves the least amount of forwarding overhead and accelerates throughput for packets that are part of an existing flow.

If the new packet does not match an entry in IPSO's connection table, then the new packet represents a new flow and requires a new connection table entry. However, if the packet matches an existing connection template, then the new connection table entry can be created; (based on information in the connection-template table entry) without a round trip to the Firewall application. The packet is then forwarded to the outbound interface for handling. This path reduces the over-head involved in creating a new connection table entry and accelerates connection rate for new connections that match existing connection templates.

If the new packet does not match an existing connection template, then a round trip to the Firewall application is required to apply the Security Policy (rules). This path involves the greatest overhead.

## VPN Capabilities

SecureXL also adds VPN routing capabilities and enhances connectivity to support VPN in dynamic routing environment, configured in SmartDashboard:

- **VPN Link Selection** — allows multiple external interfaces to be configured for tunneling the VPN packets. It allows the firewall to create, maintain, and update a table of Link Selection entries. The firewall can specify which link needs to be used for a given SA. If that link goes down, the firewall can update the Link Selection entries to start using a different link for the same tunnel.
- **Dynamic VPN Routing** — allows the VPN domain to be determined dynamically instead of configuring a static VPN domain. With Dynamic VPN routing enabled, connections can transition from clear text to encrypted or from encrypted to clear text, based on the route taken by the connection. The connection properties adapt to the route changes between an external interface (untrusted) and an internal (trusted) interface by communicating in encrypted or clear text respectively.
- **Wire Mode Connections** — allows trusted traffic to pass through without Stateful Inspection. If an internal interface is configured as wired (trusted) and the VPN community is configured as wired, then the traffic passing through the internal interface and getting encrypted using the VPN community, will skip any Stateful Inspection. This increases the connectivity at lower security for traffic between wired interfaces and a wired VPN community.

# CoreXL: Multicore Acceleration

As the first security technology to fully leverage general-purpose multi-core processors, CoreXL introduces advanced core-level load balancing that increases throughput for the deep inspection required to achieve intrusion prevention and high throughput on the firewall. With CoreXL, high performance and high security can be achieved simultaneously.

Multi-core CPU support enables Check Point Security Gateways to share traffic among cores of a single system, providing superior price/performance on a single server. The combination of multi-core CPUs and multi-threaded SecureXL security application technology is the foundation for the next generation of security acceleration-application-layer security. By joining a multi-core CPU with SecureXL security acceleration, Check Point Security Gateways can deliver more than 10 Gbps of intrusion prevention throughput.

Using CoreXL, the firewall kernel is replicated multiple times. Each replicated copy, or instance, of the firewall kernel runs on one processing core. The instances handle traffic concurrently, and each instance is a complete and independent inspection kernel. Regarding network topology, management configuration, and Security Policies, a CoreXL gateway functions as a regular Security Gateway. All of the kernel instances of a gateway handle traffic going through the same gateway interfaces and apply the same gateway Security Policy.

## Supported Platforms and Features

CoreXL does not support Check Point Suite with the following features:

- Check Point QoS (Quality of Service)
- Traffic view in SmartView Monitor (all other views are available) (supported on R75.30 and above)
- Route-based VPN
- IP Pool NAT (supported on R75.40 and above)
- IPv6 (supported on R75.40 and above)
- Firewall-1 GX
- Overlapping NAT
- SMTP resource (supported on R75.40 and above)
- VPN Traditional Mode
- VRRP

If any of the above features/settings is enabled/configured in SmartDashboard, then CoreXL acceleration will be automatically disabled on the Gateway (while CoreXL is still enabled). In order to preserve consistent configuration, before enabling one of the unsupported features, deactivate CoreXL via 'cpconfig' menu and reboot the Gateway (in cluster setup, CoreXL should be deactivated on all members).

## Default Configuration

Upon installation of CoreXL, the number of kernel instances is derived from the total number of cores in the system as described in the following table:

| Number of Cores | Number of Kernel Instances |
|---|---|
| 1 | CoreXL is disabled |
| 2 | 2 |
| 4 | 3 |
| 8 | 6 |
| More than 8 | Number of cores, minus 4 |

Table 3-1: Default Configuration

The default affinity setting for all interfaces is Automatic when Performance Pack is installed. Traffic from all interfaces is directed to the core running the Secure Network Distributor (SND).

## Processing Core Allocation

The CoreXL software architecture includes the Secure Network Distributor (SND). The SND is responsible for:

- Processing incoming traffic from the network interfaces
- Securely accelerating authorized packets (if Performance Pack is running)
- Distributing non-accelerated packets among kernel instances.

Traffic entering network interface cards (NICs) is directed to a processing core running the SND. The association of a particular interface with a processing core is called the interface's affinity with that core. This affinity causes the interface's traffic to be directed to that core and the SND to run on that core. Setting a kernel instance or a process to run on a particular core is called the instance's or process's affinity with that core.

The default affinity setting for all interfaces is Automatic. Automatic affinity means that if Performance Pack is running, the affinity for each interface is automatically reset every 60 seconds, and balanced between available cores. If Performance Pack is not running, the default affinities of all interfaces are with one available core. In both cases, any processing core running a kernel instance, or defined as the affinity for another process, is considered unavailable and will not be set as the affinity for any interface.

In some instances, SND cores can be overloaded due to high traffic on multiple interfaces assigned to the same SND core. Manual sim affinity can alleviate this symptom. Use **`sim affinity -l`** and the **`/proc/interrupts`** file to see affinity distribution. Each busy interface should be assigned its own IRQ and distributed among SND cores. Refer to sk33250 on how to edit sim affinity.

In some cases, which are discussed in the following sections, it may be advisable to change the distribution of kernel instances, the SND, and other processes, among the processing cores. This is done by changing the affinities of different NICs (interfaces) and/or processes. However, to ensure CoreXL's efficiency, all interface traffic must be directed to cores not running kernel instances. Therefore, if you change affinities of interfaces or other processes, you will need to accordingly set the number of kernel instances and ensure that the instances run on other processing cores.

Under normal circumstances, it is not recommended for the SND and an instance to share a core. However, it is necessary for the SND and an instance to share a core when using a machine with exactly two cores.

## Allocating Processing Cores

In certain cases, it may be advisable to change the distribution of kernel instances, the SND, and other processes, among the processing cores.

## Adding Processing Cores to the Hardware

Increasing the number of processing cores on the hardware platform does not automatically increase the number of kernel instances. If the number of kernel instances is not increased, CoreXL does not utilize some of the processing cores. After upgrading the hardware, increase the number of kernel instances using cpconfig.

Reinstalling the gateway will change the number of kernel instances if you have upgraded the hardware to an increased number of processing cores, or if the number of processing cores stays the same but the number of kernel instances was manually changed from the default. Use cpconfig to reconfigure the number of kernel instances.

In a clustered deployment, changing the number of kernel instances, such as by reinstalling CoreXL, should be treated as a version upgrade. Follow the instructions in the Upgrade Guide, in the "Upgrading ClusterXL Deployments" chapter, and perform either a Minimal Effort Upgrade using network downtime or a Zero Downtime Upgrade (no downtime, but active connections may be lost), substituting the instance number change for the version upgrade in the procedure. A Full Connectivity Upgrade cannot be performed when changing the number of kernel instances in a clustered environment.

## Allocating an Additional Core to the SND

In some cases, the default configuration of instances and the SND will not be optimal. If the SND is slowing the traffic, and your platform contains enough cores that you can afford to reduce the number of kernel instances, you may want to allocate an additional core to the SND. This is likely to occur especially if much of the traffic is of the type accelerated by Performance Pack; in a ClusterXL Load Sharing deployment; or if IPS features are disabled. In any of these cases, the task load of the SND may be disproportionate to that of the kernel instances.

## Allocating a Core for Heavy Logging

If the gateway is performing heavy logging, it may be advisable to allocate a processing core to the **fwd** daemon, which performs the logging. Like adding a core for the SND, this too will reduce the number of cores available for kernel instances.

## Packet Flows with SecureXL Enabled

The following image depicts packet flow through the Security Gateway when SecureXL is enabled:

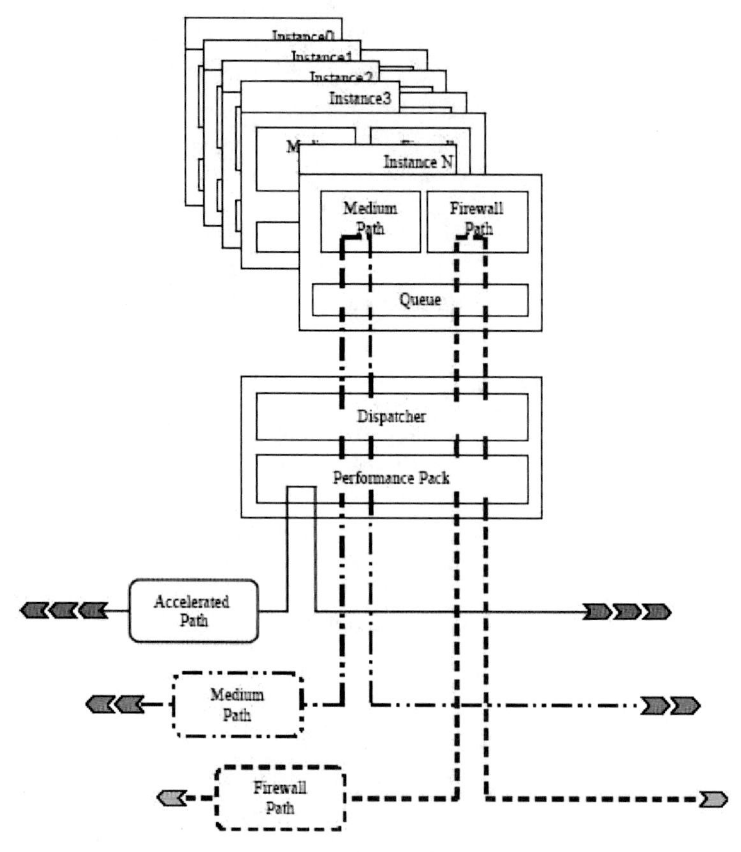


Figure 26 — Packet Flow through Security Gateway

- **Acceleration path** — The packet is completely handled by the SecureXL device. It is processed and sent back again to the network. This path does all the IPS processing when CoreXL is disabled.
- **Medium path** — The packet is handled by the SecureXL device, except for IPS processing. The CoreXL layer passes the packet to one of the firewall instances to perform IPS processing. This path is only available when CoreXL is enabled.
- **Firewall path** — The SecureXL device is unable to process the packet. It is passed on to the CoreXL layer and then to one of the instances for full firewall processing. This path also processes all packets when SecureXL is disabled.

# Practice and Review

## Practice Lab

Lab 3: Migrating to a Clustering Solution

## Review Questions

1. What is the main advantage of Monitored-circuit VRRP?

2. What two modes does State Synchronization work in?

3. What does Checkpoint recommend for securing the synchronization interfaces?

4. In a Management HA environment, how do you know when the Secondary SMS ready?

CHAPTER 4

# Advanced User Management

# *Advanced User Management*

Consistent user information is critical for proper security. Without a centralized data store, managing user information across multiple applications can be a manual, error-prone process.

## Chapter Objectives:

- Using an external user database such as LDAP, configure User Directory to incorporate user information for authentication services on the network.
- Manage internal and external user access to resources for Remote Access or across a VPN.
- Troubleshoot user access issues found when implementing Identity Awareness.

# *User Management*

Aside from knowing how to create internal users, organizing them into groups, and creating user objects to set up in a policy, it is important to administrate users authorized from a local or external database. This requires some knowledge about those databases, and then how to integrate their use with Check Point.

## Active Directory OU Structure

Active Directory is a database technology based on Lightweight Directory Access Protocol (LDAP) created by Microsoft, and is primarily used as a management tool for organizational structures in Windows environments. Active Directory is based on objects and containers set up in a hierarchical organizational structure. Each tier of the hierarchy is comprised of containers which contain objects, or a container that contain other containers and objects.

Each **object** or entry in the directory is made up of a set of attributes. An **attribute** has a name, such as an attribute type or attribute description, and one or more values. The set of rules which governs the types of objects in the directory and their associated attributes is called the **schema**. Each object has a unique identifier, its **Distinguished Name** (DN). This is its **Relative Distinguished Name** (RDN) constructed from some attribute(s) in the object, followed by the parent entry's DN.

The container in this structure is called an **Organizational Unit** or OU. OU's are tiers in the hierarchy and contain objects, which can be defined in three categories:

- **resources** — commonly defined as device objects such as printers, user PC's, and servers.
- **services** — any service that may be used within the company network, i.e. e-mail, chat, file server access.
- **users** — user accounts and their network access permissions.

Much like DNS domains, AD hierarchies are nested within each other, stemming from a root or "enterprise" level. For example, the OU *alphacorp.cp.local* will have sub-OU's such as *products.alphacorp.cp.local*, *sales.alphacorp.cp.local*, *finance.alphacorp.cp.local*, and *mis.alphacorp.cp.local*. Each of these are distinct containers at their own level, but they are all part of the enterprise container, *alphacorp.cp.local*. This extends down to the specific device object level, so that a user in MIS could have an Active Directory designation of:

*CN=Boucher,Eric,OU=MIS,DC=alphacorp,DC=cp,DC=local,* where MIS is the OU or attribute of *alphacorp.cp.local*.

The following is an example of how LDAP is commonly structured:

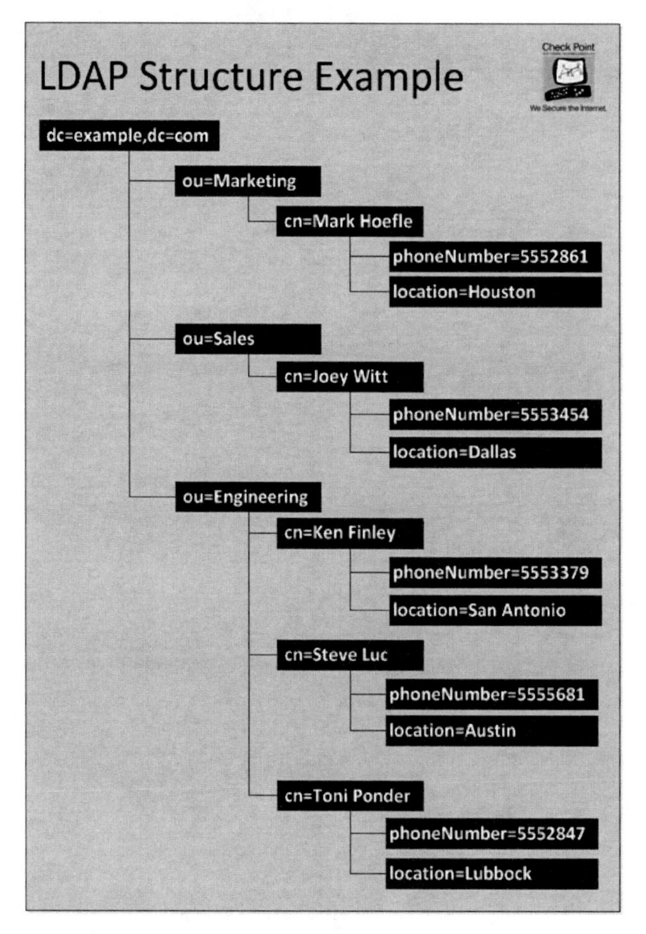


Figure 19 — LDAP Structure Example

## Using LDAP Servers with Check Point

When Check Point software is implemented, you may already have an effective user management infrastructure, such as LDAP. The Security Management Server supports LDAP technology and can use existing LDAP servers to obtain user information for authentication and authorization purposes.

If you do not have a user management infrastructure in place, you can make a choice between managing Domains on the internal users database or choosing to implement an LDAP server. If you have a large user count, it is recommended to use an external user management database, such as LDAP. By maintaining the large user database externally, the Security Management Server performance is greatly enhanced, because then the database will not have to be reinstalled every time the user information changes. Additionally, the LDAP user database can be used by other applications.

In order to manage users on a User Directory (LDAP) server a special license is required. You may choose to integrate the Security Management Server and Security Gateways with User Directory in order to:

- Query user information
- Enable User management
- Enable CRL retrieval
- Authenticate users

## LDAP User Management with User Directory

When integrated with Check Point Security Management, LDAP is referred to as **User Directory (LDAP)**. When deployed with a User Directory (LDAP) server, the Security Management Server and the Security Gateways function as User Directory (LDAP) clients, in the sense that the Security Management Server manages the user information on the User Directory (LDAP) server, and the Security Gateway will use it to query user information, retrieve CRLs and for authentication.

When incorporating LDAP users with User Directory (LDAP), it is important to understand how this is different from managing users internally. There are two main differences between user management on the internal database, and user management on a User Directory (LDAP) server. First, user management in the User Directory (LDAP) server is done externally and not locally. Second, on a User Directory (LDAP) server templates can be modified and applied to users dynamically. This means that user definitions are easy to change and to manage; and changes are instantaneous or "live". Changes that are applied to a User Directory (LDAP) template are reflected immediately for all users who are using that template.

User Directory (LDAP) features the following:

- It is based on a client/server model, in which an LDAP client makes a TCP connection to an LDAP server.
- Each entry has a unique Distinguished Name (DN).
- Default port numbers are TCP 389 for standard connections, and TCP 636 for Secure Sockets Layer (SSL) connections (LDAPS or LDAP over SSL).
- High Availability, by replicating the same information on several servers
- Compartmentalization, by allowing a large number of users to be distributed across several servers
- Encrypted and non-encrypted connections, where connections between the clients (i.e., SMS, SG) and the User Directory (LDAP) servers are conducted using SSL or in the "clear".
- Support multiple LDAP vendors using Profiles.

## Defining an Account Unit

Simply put, the Account Unit is the interface between the clients and server. Each Account Unit represents one or more branches of each User Directory (LDAP) server. Once an Account Unit is defined, it represents the location of users in the LDAP tree structure according to organization hierarchy in a corporation. For example, users in R&D may be split between developers in different product lines, but are still defined in one Account Unit, whereas another Account Unit may be defined for users in Finance even though both Account Units are associated with only one User Directory (LDAP) server.

## Configuring Active Directory

When configuring Active Directory in SmartDashboard, a User Management wizard (Identity Awareness setup) guides you through the steps. A search is made to detect any Active Directory servers on the network. If no AD server was detected, the Administrator will have the option of creating a new domain. The User Management wizard contains two parts:

- Quick setup of AD
- Users, Groups, LDAP Groups and Authentication Servers Management

## Schemas

An LDAP schema defines the types of objects and object attributes in the directory. A default schema exists which includes user definitions for that proprietary LDAP server. When all users use the same authentication scheme and are defined according to a default template, the default schema is satisfactory. But for cases where users must be defined differently, a Check Point schema can be employed. The Check Point schema complements the structure of the information in the LDAP Server, but includes Security Management Server and Security Gateway specific information as well. It can be used to enhance object definitions in the directory for more granular user authentication.

## Multiple User Directory (LDAP) Servers

Where multiple User Directory (LDAP) Servers exist in an organization, a query from one of the clients for user information is made to the servers based on a priority. This priority is defined either:

- By Gateway — Can be configured based on proximity to the LDAP server in the organization.
- By Account Unit — Has a default User Directory (LDAP) server priority list in the event a Gateway does not have a set LDAP server priority.

## Authentication Process Flow

Essentially, the authentication process begins with a fetch or query to the user database. Once the user is located, the authentication method is determined, the user is authenticated, then authorized for access.

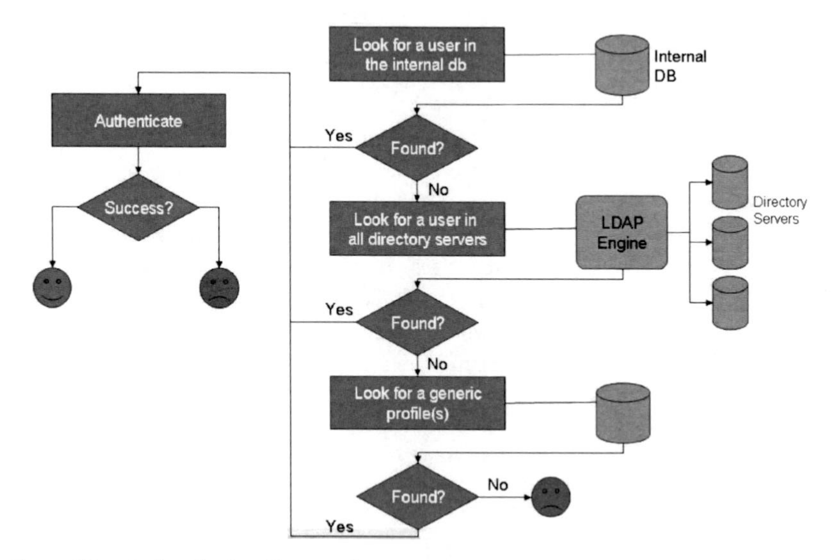


Figure 20 — Authentication Process Flow

During a query by a gateway, it will first check the internal users database. If the particular user is not defined here, the gateway will query the User Directory (LDAP) servers defined in the Account Units one at a time based on their priority. If the user is not found on one User Directory (LDAP) server, then the next one in line is queried.

If more than one Account Unit is defined on a particular User Directory (LDAP) server, then they are each queried concurrently. Results from one or more than one Account Unit may meet the conditions of the query. In this case, it will depend on gateway configuration as to which result will be applied.

If no match is found from searching the User Directory (LDAP) servers, the gateway uses the external users template to find a match based on the generic profile.

## Limitations of Authentication Flow

Though this process is very effective, there are some limitations to keep in mind. Namely:

- The authentication method is set on the user record on the internal database. In the case where an LDAP database is used, the authentication scheme cannot be set on the user record without extending the LDAP schema.
- There is a predefined search order. First the internal database is searched followed by the LDAP Servers. This slows the search down, and often results in conflicting user information.
- All the Account Units are searched simultaneously. Consequently, it cannot be determined which Account Unit to search. The different users may have the same username on different servers. However, in R75, this limitation is addressed in the gateway configuration settings.

## User Directory (LDAP) Profiles

For multi-vendor LDAP Servers, User Directory profiles are assigned to ensure that the default attributes for a given LDAP Server are properly applied. Different LDAP vendors have dissimilar object repositories, schema and object relations, and User Directory profiles are designed to normalize them for management purposes.

Four default profiles exist, and each one can be modified based on Common, Read and Write settings:

- **OPSEC_DS** — the default profile for a standard OPSEC certified User Directory (LDAP) server
- **Netscape_DS** — the profile for a Netscape Directory Server
- **Novell_DS** — the profile for a Novell Directory Server
- **Microsoft_AD** — the profile for Microsoft Active Directory.

The profile is configured whenever creating or editing an Account Unit.

## *Troubleshooting User Authentication and User Directory (LDAP)*

When encountering authentication problems for a user defined on the User Directory (LDAP) Server, first verify configuration settings:

1. Make sure that **Global properties > Smart Directory (LDAP) > Use User Directory(LDAP) for Security Gateways** is checked.
2. Verify that your AU (Account Unit) is configured for user management, i.e., **User management** is checked on the **General** tab of the AU.
3. Configure the correct User Directory profile. Which LDAP server are you using? Is it one of our supported OPSEC servers?

   Verify that your OPSEC LDAP server is supported on `http://www.opsec.com/solutions/sec_authentication.html`.
4. Check the AU object is configured correctly, i.e., profile, correct branches and administrator DN.
5. Check the LDAP group objects configuration. How did you configure the LDAP groups? If you selected the option:

   **All Account-Unit's Users** or **Only Sub Tree** - the groups defined on the LDAP server are irrelevant

   **Only Group in branch** - the group must point to a group on the LDAP server. Is it a dynamic group?
6. Where do you use authentication? The relevant LDAP groups should be used in the authorizations of the product that uses authentication. For example, when using Endpoint Connect, the user groups should be defined on the RemoteAccess object.

Once all the above are configured correctly and you have all the answers you need, obtain the following debugging information:

- Run `TDERROR_ALL_AU=5` on the process that performs the authentication. In this case, it depends on item number 4 above; for example, it would be the `vpnd` process for Endpoint Connect. Try to authenticate with the problematic user (and with a user that authenticated successfully if you have one), and save the log file.
- A capture of a successful and unsuccessful login will help you in investigating the problem, but be sure your AU object is configured not to work with SSL so that you have a clear connection. When you have the capture, try to see which attributes are being used to query for group membership.

## Common Configuration Pitfalls

When troubleshooting User Directory (LDAP) issues, the following tips are useful to keep in mind as potential causes:

- The Use User Directory (LDAP) checkbox is unchecked in Global Properties.
- Getting the bind credentials for the LDAP AU is wrong. Incorrect credentials are not flagged at the time the AU is created.
- The option, User Management is unchecked on the General tab of the AU.
- Allowed authentication schemes may be configured on the SG, but the corresponding scheme is not selected in the AU properties.
- The AUs are assigned to the SG, but the AU is not selected.
- The LDAP schema is not extended and the AU is not assigned with an authentication scheme. Even if the schema is extended, the authentication schema on the user record could still be undefined. It will remain undefined even though the AU defines a scheme.
- If the generic template is used and a password is defined on it.

## Some LDAP Tools

For tools on the firewall, refer to:

- **ldapsearch**

  For example: **ldapsearch -D cn=administrator,cn=users,dc=boaz,dc=com -w zuburl! -b cn=users,dc=boaz,dc=com -h 20.20.20.100 '(&(objectclass=user)(sAMAccountName=zaza) )' mobile otherMobile**
- **ldapcmd** (per process, commands: **cacheclear**, **cachetrace**, **log on/off**)
- **ldapmodify**

  For example: **ldapmodify -c -h <host> -D <Admin FQDN> -w <password> -f <schema ldif file>**

## Troubleshooting User Authentication

A set of libraries in the **/CPShared** directory is linked to the application process. The processes which perform the authentication include:

- fwm - SmartDashboard authentication
- vpnd - Remote Access authentication
- cvpnd - SSL VPN user authentication
- Security Servers - user/client/session authentications

In addition, while the actual authorization is performed by the application, the authentication is mostly performed by the infrastructure in cpauth. The authentication infrastructure code modules in the chain include:

- cpauth

  The authentication schemes performed by cpauth include:

  Username and password (internal database as well as LDAP)

  RADIUS

  SecurID

  TACACS

  OS password
- cpldapcl, ldap
- ace5sdk

In addition, when examining log entries, search for the following information to help with the debugging:

- Username
- Functions: **make_au**, **au_auth**, **au_fetchuser**, **cpLdapGetUser**, **cpLdapCheck**
- After fetch the user's set is printed
- Auth starts with **au_auth_auth**, look for the authentication result
- Often the problem is authorization, not authentication

# *Identity Awareness*

This section devotes attention to troubleshooting Identity Awareness to address a typical network security expert's job task requirements. Advanced User Management must take into account this product because of its importance in controlling corporate resources and increased visibility of user activities.

Identity Awareness includes these key features:

- **Configurable access roles** — Use the Identity Awareness software blade to easily add users, user-groups and machine identity intelligence to your security defenses. This information is obtained from the corporate directory services.
- **Multiple user identification methods** — Provides multiple methods to obtain a user's identity; Clientless, Captive Portal or Light Agent. Identity information can be utilized by relevant software blades to apply and enforce user-based policies.
- **Deployment wizard for fast & simple deployment** — Adding identity intelligence via the Identity Awareness Software Blade is fast and easy with the built in deployment wizard. In a few steps user, user-group, and machine information can be made available to utilize in policies throughout the security infrastructure.
- **Identity sharing** — Identity information can easily be shared as required, on a single gateway or across the entire network. In a multiple gateway deployment, such as multiple branches or multiple gateways protecting internal resources, identity can be acquired on one gateway and shared among all gateways.

Identity Awareness uses IP addresses, normally reserved by the Firewall to monitor traffic as a means to map users and machine identities.

Identity Awareness acquires user identities in several methods referred to as **Identity Sources**, which include AD Query, Captive Portal, and Light Agent. For troubleshooting purposes, we will focus on two types:

- **AD Query** identifies users logged on to Active Directory without prompting users for installation or credentials.
- **Captive Portal** (browser based authentication) identifies users by sending them to a Web page for authentication with Active Directory or other LDAP servers.

Once you enable an identity source on the gateway, the gateway will map IP addresses in your network to the respective user active for each IP. When traffic arrives from/to the IPs, the gateway will include the user and computer name in the logs.

The following information provides some tips for troubleshooting cases when Identity Awareness cannot identify users in your network, and when traffic logs do not contain user information.

The troubleshooting procedure includes:

1. Verifying AD Query Setup
2. Identifying users behind an HTTP proxy
3. Verifying there's a logged on AD user in the source IP
4. Checking the source computer OS and activating captive portal
5. Using SmartView Tracker for further troubleshooting

## Enabling AD Query

Once you enable AD Query on a gateway, the gateway will register to the configured domain controllers in order to receive security event logs. By analyzing these logs, the gateway will map IPs on your network to their respective users and computers.

AD Query does not detect all users and computers immediately. Depending on the activity in your network, AD Query may take up to a few hours to complete the mapping of users and computers to IPs.

To quickly identify a user, lock the user computer, wait a few seconds and then unlock it. This will generate a security event log and mapping of the user name to the IP will take place.

## AD Query Setup

In addition to enabling AD Query in your policy, verify that the following conditions are met:

- Active Directory event logging is setup.

  Verify that domain controllers are configured to audit authentication success events. This is the default behavior in AD but may have been changed in your organization. In the domain controller Event Viewer, look for the following event numbers:
- Windows 2003: events 672, 673 and 674.
- Windows 2008: events 4624, 4768, 4769 and 4770.
- The LDAP Account Unit is setup.

  Verify that all domain controllers to which users authenticate are configured in the LDAP Account Unit Servers list. The Security Event log is not synchronized between domain controllers.
- The gateway successfully connects to all domain controllers.

  Use SmartView Monitor to see the status of connections to domain controllers or run "adlog a dc" in expert mode on the gateway to see connection status from the gateway to domain controllers. Typical reasons for *lack* of connectivity to domain controller:

  - A firewall/IPS device en route to the domain controller is blocking DCOM (port 135 or high port used by DCOM).
  - Check Point Firewall or IPS may be blocking DCOM. See SK 58881 for resolution.
- Non-English user names: To support non-English user names, you must set an attribute using dbedit or GuiDBEdit. Set the **SupportUnicode** attribute to **true** on the LDAP Account Unit object. The LDAP Account Unit object is found in the Servers table.
- That users reach the gateway and domain controller with the same endpoint IP.

Users will reach the gateway with a different IP in the following cases:

- When there's a NAT device between the users and the AD domain controller or gateway.
- When users connect through a Citrix or Terminal Server.
- When many users authenticate to one server such as Outlook Web access server.

Users connecting behind NAT or via Citrix or Terminal Servers are supported via an agent. When AD Query detects 7 or more users on the same IP, this IP is disregarded.

## Identifying users behind an HTTP proxy

If your organization uses an HTTP proxy server positioned between users and the Security Gateway, logs will show the proxy as their source IP address and will not show the user's identity. For Application Control, the gateway can use the X-Forward-For HTTP header, which is added by the proxy server, to resolve this issue.

To use X-Forwarded-For HTTP header with Application Control:

1. Configure your proxy server to use X-Forwarded-For HTTP Header.
2. In SmartDashboard, on the Identity Awareness page of the gateway object, check "For Application Control blade, detect users located behind HTTP proxy using X-Forwarded-For header".
3. Install the policy.

## Verifying there's a logged on AD user at the source IP

Once you verified the conditions in "AD Query Setup" are met, the next step is to verify that the computer on the IP in question is a domain computer and there's a user logged on.

To verify that the source IP is indeed of an AD user:

1. Verify the computer is a domain member. From a computer in the domain, try to access the `C$` share on the source IP. For example, using the **`Start->Run`** command, enter `\\10.0.0.1\C$`. When prompted for credentials, enter a domain administrator credentials. If you successfully opened the `C$` share it means this is a domain computer.
2. Verify that there's a user logged on. Use a WMI tool such as WMI Explorer to remotely connect to the IP and query for the user name.

## Checking the source computer OS

If you cannot connect to the source IP **C$** share or with WMI Explorer, it is likely that this IP is a computer that is not a member of the domain. It is also possible but less likely, that this IP is a domain computer but RPC and WMI traffic is blocked in your network or on the target computer.

To help determine the OS at the IP, use remote endpoint profiling tools such as **nmap** to detect the OS. For example run "**nmap -A 10.0.0.1**" to detect the OS on this IP:

```
D:\Tools\nmap-5.21>nmap -A 10.0.0.1

Starting Nmap 5.21 ( http://nmap.org ) at 2010-12-19 13:00 Jerusalem Standard Time
Nmap scan report for 91.90.139.49
Host is up (0.14s latency).
Not shown: 993 closed ports
PORT      STATE    SERVICE        VERSION
135/tcp   open     msrpc          Microsoft Windows RPC
445/tcp   open     netbios-ssn
3389/tcp  open     ms-term-serv?
5357/tcp  open     http           Microsoft HTTPAPI httpd 2.0 (SSDP/UPnP)
|_html-title: Service Unavailable
49152/tcp filtered unknown
49153/tcp open     msrpc          Microsoft Windows RPC
49154/tcp open     msrpc          Microsoft Windows RPC
MAC Address: 00:21:86:ED:D0:2C (USI)
No exact OS matches for host (If you know what OS is running on it, see http://nmap.o
TCP/IP fingerprint:
OS:SCAN(V=5.21%D=12/19%OT=135%CT=1%CU=41592%PV=N%DS=1%DC=D%G=Y%M=002186%TM=
OS:4D0DE65A%P=i686-pc-windows-windows)SEQ(SP=103%GCD=1%ISR=106%TI=I%CI=I%II
OS:=I%SS=S%TS=7)SEQ(SP=106%GCD=2%ISR=107%TI=I%CI=I%II=I%SS=S%TS=7)SEQ(SP=10
OS:5%GCD=1%ISR=107%TI=I%CI=I%II=I%SS=S%TS=7)SEQ(SP=106%GCD=1%ISR=108%TI=I%C
OS:I=I%II=I%SS=S%TS=7)OPS(O1=M5B4NW8ST11%O2=M5B4NW8ST11%O3=M5B4NW8NNT11%O4=

Network Distance: 1 hop
Service Info: OS: Windows

HOP RTT       ADDRESS
1   144.00 ms 91.90.139.49

OS and Service detection performed. Please report any incorrect results at http://nma
Nmap done: 1 IP address (1 host up) scanned in 124.65 seconds
```

Figure 21 — nmap Example

If this is not a Windows computer, turn on the captive portal on the gateway so that Web traffic will be intercepted and the user will have to authenticate. (The AD Query identifies computers logged on the domain.)

## Using Smartview Tracker

When you've verified that the source IP belongs to an AD user and the conditions described in "AD Query Setup" are met, but traffic logs still don't contain this user, you can track the Identity Awareness Login Activity in order to further troubleshoot the cause.

1. Open SmartView Tracker Identity Awareness Login Activity view.
2. Search for log records from the user that's missing in logs.

   Login logs (green door) and Logout logs (grey door) will be displayed.
3. Follow the steps below to find the possible cause of the missing users:

   — If you see no Login logs, try searching in log files that have been switched already (SmartView Tracker will open the active log files). If you still see no logs, it means that AD Query failed to identify the user and you should contact support.

   — If you see Login logs and AD Query runs on a different gateway (not the one that generated the traffic log), verify that identity sharing is configured correctly in the Identity Awareness properties.

   — In the Identity Sharing properties of the gateway that generates the logs, verify that it gets identities from **All sharing gateways** or specifically from the gateway that runs AD Query. In the Identity Sharing properties of the gateway that runs AD Query, verify that **Share local identities with other gateways** is checked.

   If you see Logout logs despite the fact that the user was active in the duration following the Login log, try to increase the AD Query association time-out. This time-out is 12 hours by default but if it's lowered, users will be detected as logged out sooner. (When using AD Query, Logout occurs when no security event logs are created for a user for 10 hours by default).

   — If you see a Logout log of the user followed by a Login log of a different user on the same IP, then it's possible that there is a Windows service that logs on with a user account.

   By default, AD Query will aggregate the 2 or more users on the IP unless you checked the **Assume that only one user is connected per computer** option, in which case the service will cause the user account to be logged out.

   To deal with this scenario, enter the account used by the service in the **Excluded Users/Machines** list found in AD Query Advanced Settings.

# Practice and Review

## Practice Lab

Lab 4: Configuring SmartDashboard to Interface with Active Directory

## Review Questions

1. What objects make up an Organizational Unit container?

2. What does an LDAP Schema do?

3. What long does it take for an AD Query to map users and computers to IPs?

4. If you cannot connect to the source IP **C$** share or with WMI Explorer, what is the likely cause?

CHAPTER 5

# *Advanced IPsec VPN and Remote Access*

# *Advanced IPsec VPN and Remote Access*

Check Point's VPN Software Blade is an integrated software solution that provides secure connectivity to corporate networks, remote and mobile users, branch offices and business partners. The blade integrates access control, authentication and encryption to guarantee the security of network connections over the public Internet.

## Objectives

- Using your knowledge of fundamental VPN tunnel concepts, troubleshoot a site-to-site or certificate-based VPN on a corporate gateway using IKEView, VPN log files and command-line debug tools.
- Optimize VPN performance and availability by using Link Selection and Multiple Entry Point solutions.
- Manage and test corporate VPN tunnels to allow for greater monitoring and scalability with multiple tunnels defined in a community including other VPN providers.

# *Advanced VPN Concepts and Practices*

As a network security expert, working with VPNs is fundamental to your typical tasks and job responsibilities, requiring an in-depth working knowledge of VPN technology and concepts. This chapter assumes a basic comprehension of encryption, cryptography applications (algorithms and hash methods), and configuration of site-to-site VPNs using either pre-shared secrets or Certificates.

## IPsec

IPsec is an open standard protocol suite for secure IP communications using authentication and encryption techniques on IP packets. The following are used to perform various functions:

- **Encapsulating Security Payloads (ESP)** — provides confidentiality, data origin authentication, connection less integrity, an anti-replay service, and limited traffic flow confidentiality.
- **Security Associations (SA)** — though not a protocol, this data structure provides the bundle of algorithms and data that are the parameters necessary to operate the AH and/or ESP operations.

## Internet Key Exchange (IKE)

It is the Security Associations that provides the set of algorithms and data that establish the parameters to use AH and ESP. The SA provides the necessary framework for authentication and key exchange, so that the actual Internet Key Exchange (IKE) protocol can provide the authenticated keying material. The encrypted traffic flows unidirectionally, so a pair of SAs is required to form a tunnel that is bidirectional.

IKE negotiation consists of two phases, Phase 1 (Main mode), and Phase 2 (Quick mode). The negotiation process in both modes can be observed in **`ike.elg`** with an internal Check Point utility called IKEview. We will cover guidelines for analyzing **`ike.elg`**, and instructions for collecting **`ike.elg`** and **`vpnd.elg`** data.

This section discusses only IKEv1 and not Aggressive Mode. While Aggressive Mode is preferred by some third party gateways, its use is discouraged for Check Point configurations unless required in your production environment.

## IKE Key Exchange Process - Phase 1

Troubleshooting a VPN requires an understanding of the process of creating a VPN tunnel. The following is the IKE exchange process.

**Phase 1** (Main mode) negotiates encryption methods, (i.e. AES, 3DES, etc.), the hash algorithm (SHA1 and MD5), and establishes a key to protect messages of an exchange. The following describes the stages of the Phase 1 process:

**Stage 1**: Peers negotiate algorithms, authentication methods, and Diffie-Hellman (DH) groups.
**Stage 2**: Each gateway generates a DH private key and public keys and calculate the shared keys.
**Stage 3**: Peers authenticate using the certificate or PSK.

Example: The IKE exchange uses six packets for Phase 1 (Main mode) and three packets for Phase 2 (Quick mode): For Main mode packet 1, the initiator 172.24.104.1 provides the following information:

- Encryption algorithm: AES-CBC
- Key length: 256 bit
- Hash algorithm: SHA1
- Authentication method: pre-shared key

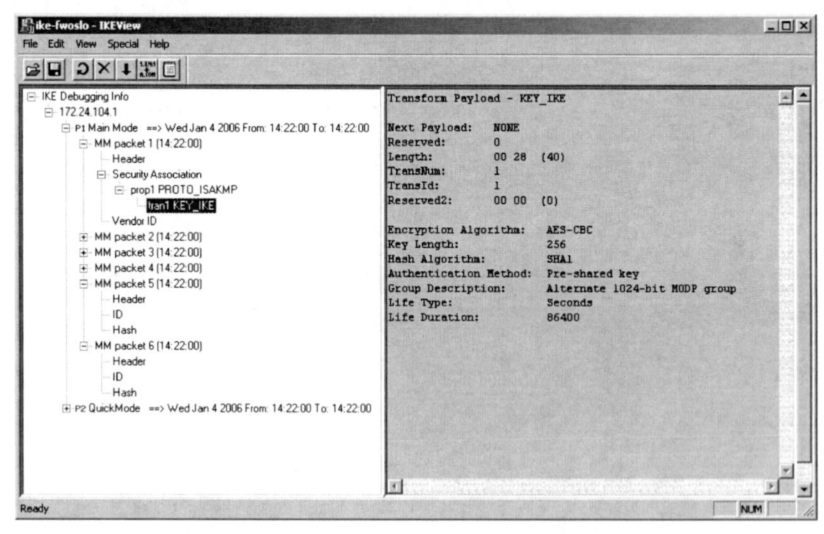


Figure 22 — IKEView

1. Packet 2 is from the responder to agree on one encryption and hash algorithm:

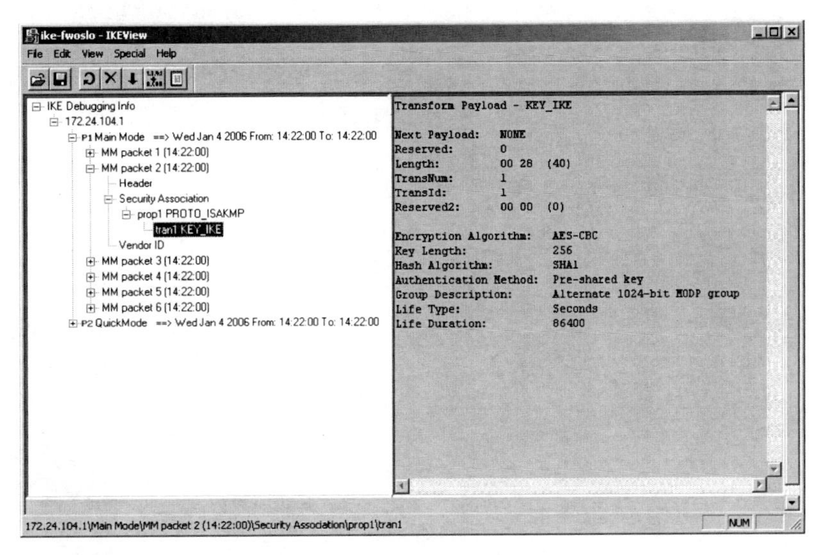


Figure 23 — Packet 2

2. Packets 3 and 4 perform key exchanges and include a large number never used before, called a nonce. A nonce is a set of random numbers sent to the other party, signed and returned to prove the party's identity. These two packets are not generally used in troubleshooting a key exchange with IKEview.

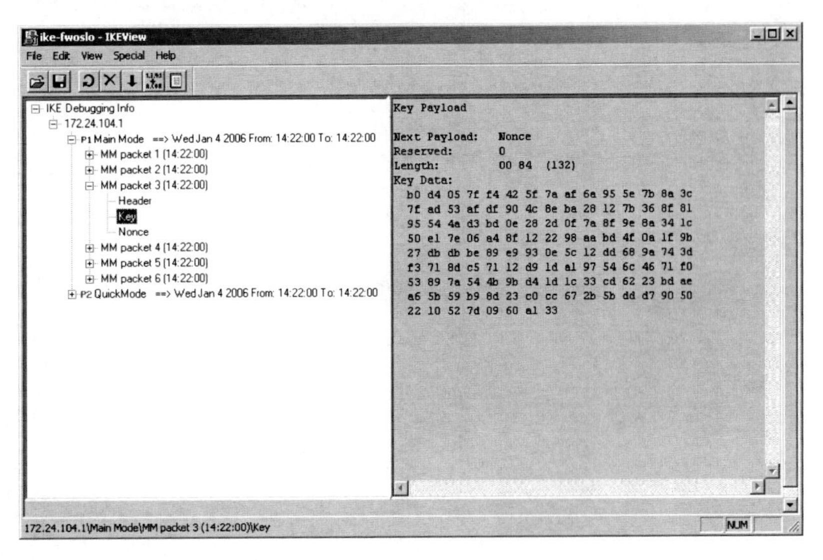


Figure 24 — Packets 3 and 4

3. Packets 5 and 6 perform authentication between the peers of the tunnel. The peer's IP address shows in the ID field under MM packet 5:

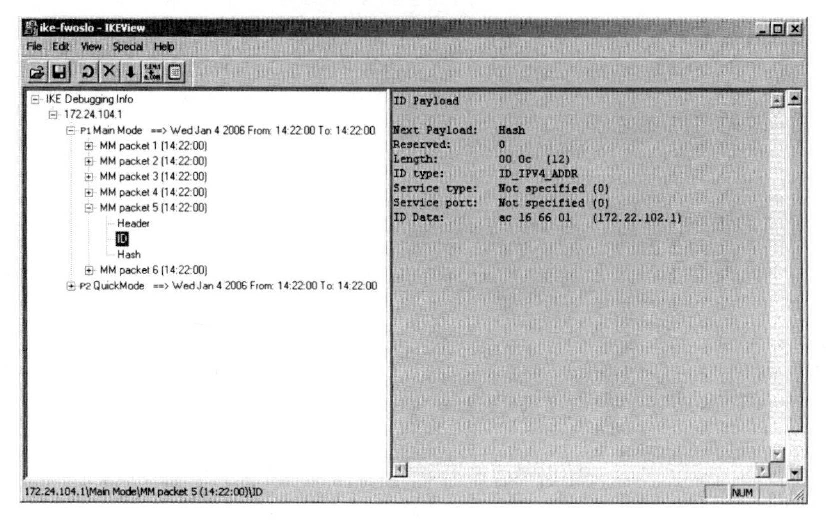


Figure 25 — Packets 5 and 6

4. Packet 6 shows the peer has agreed to the proposal and has authenticated the initiator:

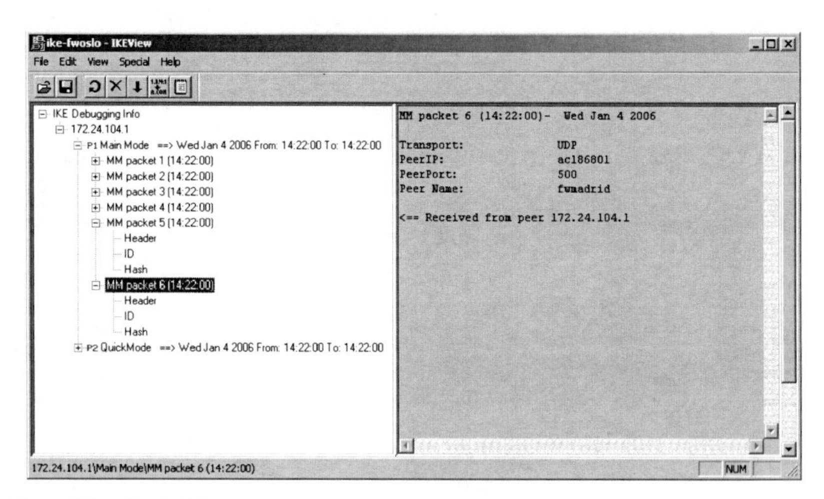


Figure 26 — Packet 6

In Phase 2, the IPsec Security Associations (SAs) are negotiated, the shared-secret key material used for security algorithms is determined, and an additional DH exchange occurs. Phase 2 failures are frequently due to a misconfigured VPN Domain, which could include omitted objects, duplicated objects or choosing all IP addresses behind the Security Gateway. Typically, Check Point recommends a manually defined VPN Domain, which includes all network objects that will participate in the VPN communication.

## Phase 2 Stages

Phase 2 can be broken into the following general stages:

- Peers exchange more key material, and agree on encryption and integrity methods for IPSec.
- The DH key is combined with the key material to produce the symmetrical IPSec key.
- Symmetric IPSec keys are generated.

The following steps detail the Phase 2 stages:

1. Packet 1 proposes either a subnet or host ID, an encryption and hash algorithm, and ID data:

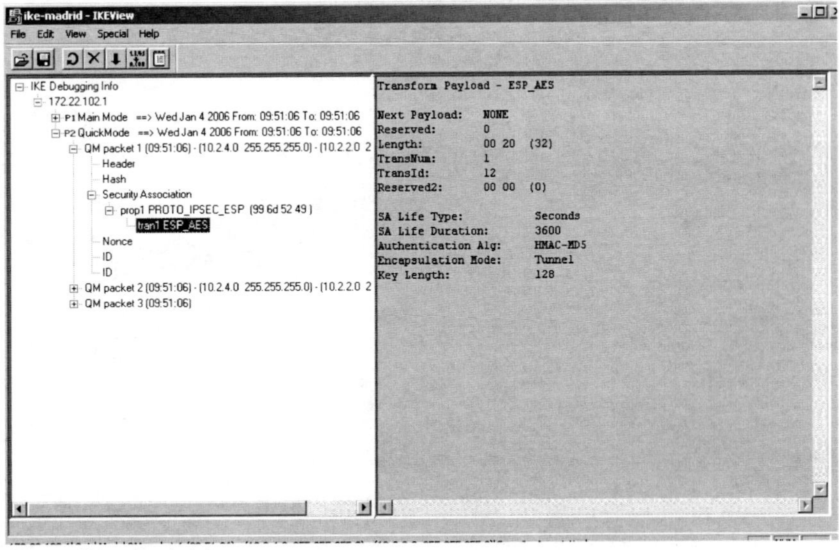


Figure 27 — Packet 1

In the ID field, the initiator's VPN Domain configuration displays. In the following figure, the VPN Domain for the initiator is the 10.2.4.0/24 network:

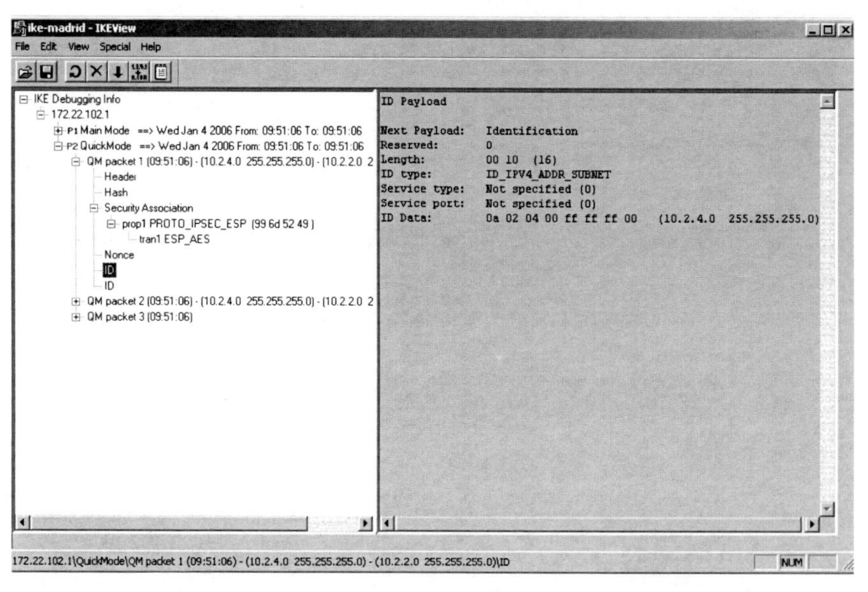


Figure 28 — VPN Domain

2. ID field_2 proposes the peer's VPN Domain configuration. In the figure below, the VPN Domain for the peer Gateway is the 10.2.2.0/24 network:

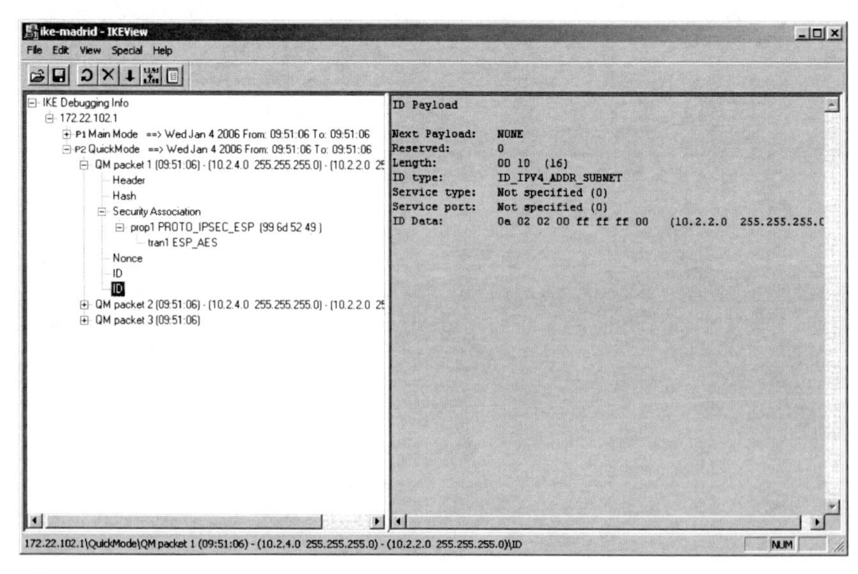


Figure 29 — VPN Domain

3. Packet 2 from the responder agrees to its own subnet or host ID, and encryption and hash algorithm:

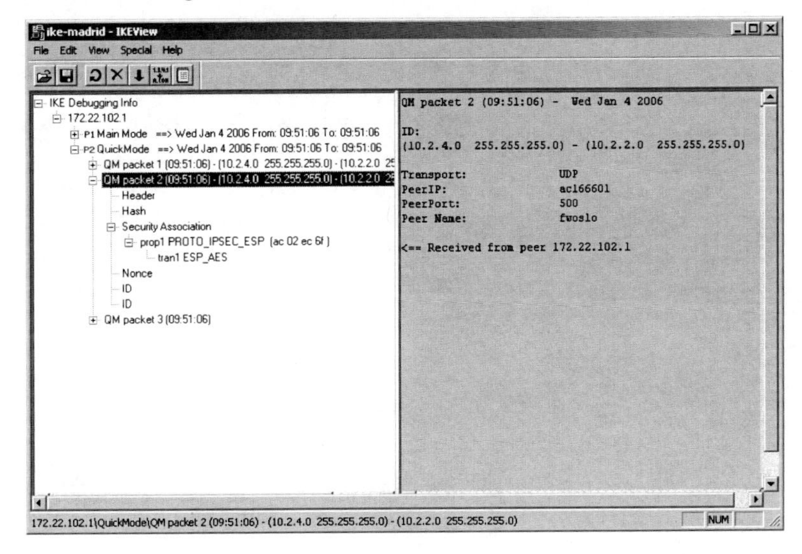


Figure 30 — Packet 2

4. Packet 3 completes the IKE negotiation:

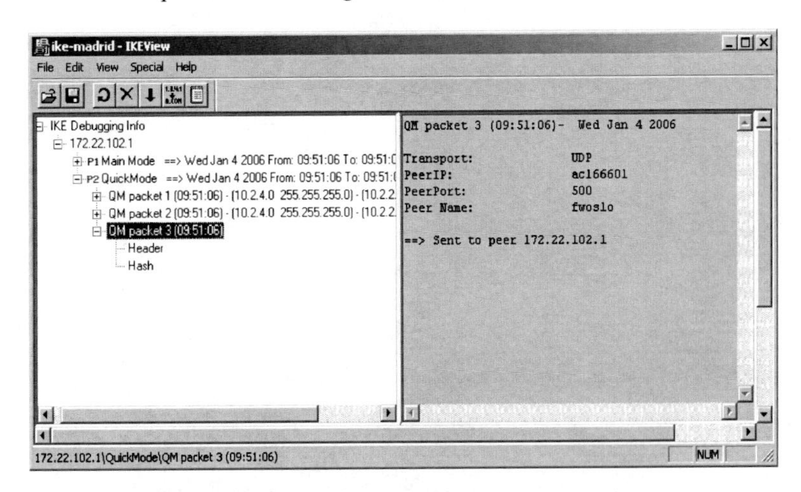


Figure 31 — Packet 3

# Remote Access VPNs

Aside from the site-to-site and certificate-based VPNs, Check Point provides several Remote-Access VPN solutions that enable VPN tunnel creation between remote users and an organization's internal network. The most recent of these is Endpoint Connect, which is a lightweight remote access client supplying secure IPsec VPN connectivity to resources on the client machine. It is designed so that the native desktop is used to launch business applications rather than through a mobile access portal. Unlike SecuRemote/SecureClient remote access solutions, Endpoint Connect does not require authentication each time a connection is initiated.

## Connection Initiation

In order for a VPN tunnel to be established between the site (Security Gateway) and a remote user, an IKE negotiation must take place between them. The peer identities are authenticated (phase 1), where the gateway and client each verify the other's identity. Authentication is performed using:

- Digital Certificates
- Pre-Shared Secrets
- Hybrid Mode
  - One-Time Password
  - Security Gateway Password
  - OS Password
  - RADIUS
  - TACACS
  - SAA

Once authentication is successful, the final IKE negotiation is attempted (phase 2), and the VPN tunnel is established.

However, in order for encrypted connections to exist for SecuRemote/SecureClient remote users, the organization's internal network (topology) must be known. The Security Gateway downloads this information which includes IP addresses of network resources and host addresses of other Security Gateways that are part of the VPN domain. This topology information, along with client configuration properties, is downloaded to the client over a secured connection using SSL over IKE.

The connection type in which a client connects with the gateway is called the Connect Mode. The initial connection is made directly to the gateway, but all subsequent connections to internal resources will be made through transparently initiated VPN links. Recall that there are five connection methods which can be used separately, or together:

- **Office Mode** — Where a Gateway assigns a remote client an IP address after connection and authentication takes place.
- **Visitor Mode** — When the client needs to have a tunnel to the gateway site through a TCP connection on port 443.
- **Hub Mode** — Where all traffic is routed through the Security Gateway
- **Auto connect** — When an application tries to open a connection to a host behind a gateway, SecureClient will prompt the user to open a tunnel to that gateway.
- **User Profiles** — Different user profiles are used to overcome changing connectivity conditions, for example, a profile that enables Visitor mode when the remote client must tunnel the VPN connection over port 443.

## Link Selection

There are times when having more control over VPN traffic is useful, particularly when high-traffic demands are applied to the gateway and its performance is impaired. Link Selection provides the means to specify which interfaces are to be used for incoming and outgoing VPN traffic. The Administrator can also choose the IP addresses used for VPN traffic on each Security Gateway.

Among the configuration options, the administrator can choose to:

- Probe links for availability
- Use Load Sharing on links to distribute VPN traffic
- Use links based on services to control the bandwidth
- Set up links for remote access

Link Selection is configured in Security **Gateway Properties > IPSec VPN > Link Selection**. For more details about these settings, refer to the R75 VPN Administration Guide.

Link Selection is only applicable to locally managed VPN peers, such as Endpoint Connect users, or other gateways configured for VPN traffic as long as they are managed centrally by the same Management Server or CMA (see Multi-Domain Security Management).

If the link is set to the wrong IP address, VPN connectivity configured for a remote site can be damaged, unless it is configured to "auto-probe". For example, assume a client creates a site with the external IP address of the gateway. During the creation process, the topology is downloaded, including the link selection IP, which was set to the internal interface of the gateway. From that point, the client will attempt to establish a tunnel with the IP address set in the Link Selection settings (the internal IP address), instead of the pre-configured external IP selected during site creation. In this case, the connection to the site will most likely fail.

# Multiple Entry Point VPNs

If a single gateway provides access to internal resources for remote VPN connections, then access to valuable resources to remote users is vulnerable should the gateway become unavailable. A Multiple Entry Point (MEP) solution was devised to provide an HA solution for VPNs. However, unlike Clustered gateways:

- MEP VPNs are not restricted to the location of gateways.
- MEP Security Gateways can be managed by separate Management Servers.
- There is no state synchronization needed between gateways. If one MEP gateway fails, the current connection is lost, but another MEP gateway picks up the next connection.
- The VPN client selects which Gateway site will take over the connection should the first fail; clustered Gateways make the selection themselves in a ClusterXL deployment.

## How Does MEP Work

MEP VPNs use the proprietary Probing Protocol (PP) to send special UDP RDP packets to port 259 to discover whether a location (IP) is reachable. It is used by the peer to continuously probe all MEP Security Gateways. The probe will indicate if a gateway is available or not. In this way, each MEP gateway shares its status with the others, and updates each should conditions change.

## Explicit MEP

Only Star VPN Communities using more than one central Security Gateway can be defined explicitly as MEP VPNs. This is the recommended method. Explicit MEP VPNs can be configured to have the entry-point Security Gateway chosen either by:

- Selecting the closest gateway to the source (First to respond)
- Selecting the closest gateway to the destination (By VPN domain)
- Selecting randomly (for Load distribution)
- Selecting from a priority list (MEP rules)

## Implicit MEP

If fully or partially overlapping encryption domains exist, or where primary or backup gateways are configured, then the MEP VPNs can be implicitly defined. Implicit MEP VPNs can be configured to have the entry-point Security Gateway selected either by:

- **First to respond** — When no primary Security Gateway is available, all gateways have equal priority, and the first gateway to respond to the probing RDP packets gets chosen as the entry point. Usually, that means the gateway closest to the remote VPN peer in proximity.
- **Primary-Backup** — If the primary Security Gateway fails, VPN connectivity is made to go through the backup gateway.
- **Load Distribution** — If all the Security Gateways share equal priority and the same VPN domain, the traffic load can be distributed so that the connections are shared evenly between all the gateways.

For remote access MEP VPNs, each client must use Office mode and assigned its own pool of addresses. If the clients are connected via a routing backbone, then each pool must be routed to the appropriate site. If the client is connected via site-to-site, then it needs to be included in the encryption domain of each gateway.

# Tunnel Management

There are two types of VPN tunnel management:

- **Permanent Tunnels** — This feature keeps VPN tunnels active, allowing real-time monitoring capabilities.
- **VPN Tunnel Sharing** — This feature provides greater interoperability and scalability between Gateways. It also controls the number of VPN tunnels created between peer Gateways.

## Permanent Tunnels

As companies have become more dependent on VPNs for communication to other sites, uninterrupted connectivity has become more crucial than ever before. It is essential to make sure VPN tunnels are kept up and running. Permanent Tunnels are constantly kept active, and as a result, make it easier to recognize malfunctions and connectivity problems. Security Administrators can monitor the two sides of a VPN tunnel, and identify problems without delay. Each VPN tunnel in a Community may be set to be a Permanent Tunnel.

Since Permanent Tunnels are constantly monitored, if a VPN tunnel fails for some reason, a log, alert, or user-defined action can be issued. A VPN tunnel is monitored by periodically sending tunnel-test packets. As long as responses to the packets are received, the VPN tunnel is considered “up”. If no response is received within a given time period, the VPN tunnel is considered “down”.

Permanent Tunnels can only be established between Check Point Gateways. The configuration of Permanent Tunnels takes place on Community objects. There are three options to configure a Permanent Tunnel:

- **For the entire Community** — this option sets every VPN tunnel in the Community as permanent.
- **For a specific Gateway** — use this option to configure specific Gateways to have Permanent Tunnels.
- **For a single VPN tunnel** — this feature allows configuring specific tunnels between specific Gateways as permanent.

## Tunnel Testing

Tunnel Test is a proprietary Check Point protocol that is used to test whether VPN tunnels are working. A tunnel-test packet has an arbitrary length, with only the first byte containing meaningful data — the type field.

The type field can take any of the following values:

1 - Test
2 - Reply
3 - Connect
4 - Connected

Tunnel testing requires two Gateways, one configured as a "Pinger" and one as a "responder". The Pinger Gateway uses the VPN daemon (vpnd) to send encrypted tunnel-testing packets to the responder Gateway. The responder Gateway is configured to listen on port 18234 for special tunnel-testing packets. The Pinger sends type 1 or 3. The responder sends a packet of identical length, with type 2 or 4 respectively. During the connect phase, tunnel testing is used in two ways:

- A connect message is sent to the Gateway. Receipt of a connect message is the indication that the connection succeeded. Connect messages are retransmitted for up to 10 seconds after the IKE negotiation is over, if no response is received.
- A series of test messages with various lengths is sent, so as to discover the Path Maximum Transmission Unit (PMTU) of the connection. This may also take up to 10 seconds. This test is executed to ensure that TCP packets that are too large are not sent. TCP packets that are too large will be fragmented and slow down performance.

## VPN Tunnel Sharing

Since various vendors implement IPSec tunnels in a number of different methods, Administrators need to cope with different means of implementing the IPSec framework. VPN Tunnel Sharing provides interoperability and scalability, by controlling the number of VPN tunnels created between peer Gateways. There are three available settings:

- One VPN Tunnel per each pair of hosts
- One VPN Tunnel per subnet pair
- One VPN Tunnel per Gateway pair

## Tunnel-Management Configuration

Tunnel management is configured in the community object:

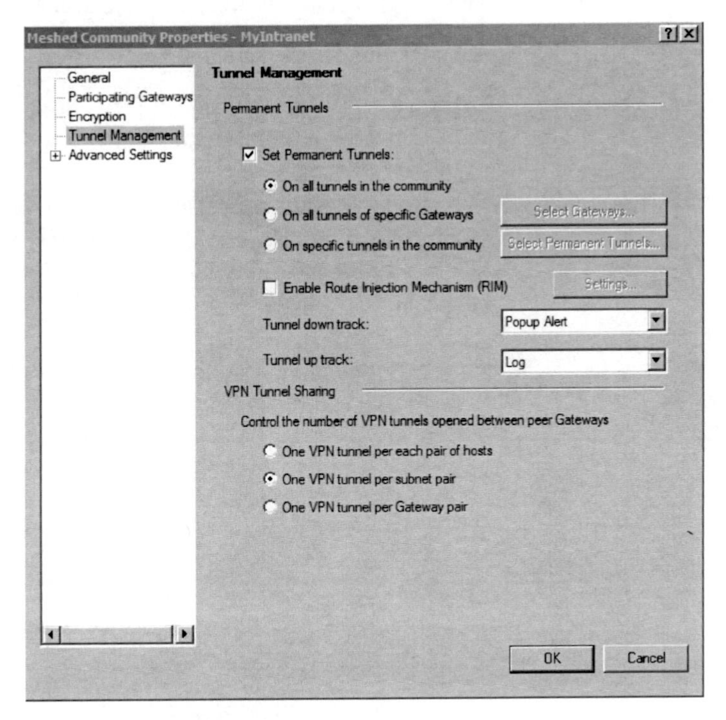


Figure 32 — Tunnel Management

## Permanent-Tunnel Configuration

To set VPN tunnels as permanent, select **Set Permanent Tunnels**. The following Permanent Tunnel modes are then made available:

- On all tunnels in the community
- On all tunnels of specific Gateways
- On specific tunnels in the community

To make all VPN tunnels permanent in a Community, select **On all tunnels in the community**. To make all VPN tunnels of specific Gateways permanent, select **On all tunnels of specific Gateways**. Select the specific Gateways you want, and all VPN tunnels to the specific Gateway will be set as permanent.

Tracking options can be configured for specific Gateways' VPN tunnels in the Gateway tunnels properties screen. Use Community Tracking Option as the default setting. You can select specific tracking options:

To configure specific tunnels in a Community to be permanent, select **On specific Tunnels** in the community. Click the **Set Permanent Tunnels** button.

For example, to make the tunnel between Remote-1-gw and Remote-3-gw permanent, click in the cell that intersects the Remote-1-gw and Remote-3-gw where a permanent tunnel is required.

1. Click **Selected Tunnel Properties** to display the Tunnel Properties screen:
2. Click **Select these tunnels to be permanent tunnels**.
3. Click **OK**.

## Tracking options

Several types of alerts can be configured to keep Administrators up-to-date on the status of VPN tunnels. Tracking settings can be configured on the Tunnel Management screen of the Community Properties window for all VPN tunnels, or they can be set individually when configuring the permanent tunnels themselves. The different options are Log, Popup Alert, Mail Alert, SNMP Trap Alert, and User Defined Alert. Choosing one of these alert types will enable immediate identification of the problem and the ability to respond to these issues more effectively.

## Advanced Permanent-Tunnel Configuration

Several attributes allow for customization of tunnel tests and intervals for permanent tunnels:

1. In SmartDashboard, select **Global Properties** > **SmartDashboard Customization**.
2. Click **Configure**. The Advanced configuration screen is displayed.
3. Click **VPN Advanced Properties** > **Tunnel Management** to view the five attributes.

## VPN Tunnel Sharing Configuration

VPN Tunnel Sharing provides greater interoperability and scalability, by controlling the number of VPN tunnels created between peer Gateways.

Configuration of VPN Tunnel Sharing can be set on both the VPN community and Gateway objects. Tunnel Sharing is configured using the following settings:

- One VPN tunnel per each pair of hosts; A VPN tunnel is created for every session initiated between every pair of hosts.
- One VPN tunnel per subnet pair; Once a VPN tunnel has been opened between two subnets, subsequent sessions between the same subnets will share the same VPN tunnel. This is the default setting, and is compliant with the IPSec industry standard.
- One VPN tunnel per Gateway pair; One VPN tunnel is created between peer Gateways and shared by all hosts behind each peer Gateway.

If there is a conflict between the tunnel properties of a VPN Community and a Gateway object that is a member of that same Community, the "stricter" setting is used. For example, a Gateway object that was set to one VPN Tunnel per each pair of hosts, and a community object that was set to one VPN Tunnel per subnet pair, VPN sharing, will use one VPN Tunnel per each pair of hosts.

## *Troubleshooting*

The first step in troubleshooting a VPN tunnel and IKE negotiation is to ensure packets destined for the VPN tunnel from the peer arrive at the Security Gateway, and vice versa. The SmartView Tracker log is a good way to confirm that IKE packets arrive at the Gateway. If there are no messages in SmartView Tracker, **`fw monitor`** is helpful for confirming if IKE packets arrive and leave the Gateway.

Once you verify IKE packets arrive at both sides, run a debug for IKE traffic with the **`vpn debug on`** command. Generate some traffic from your VPN Domain to the peer's VPN Domain. If the **`ike.elg`** file does not contain useful information, an invalid tunnel may have been initiated previously, and it is necessary to remove related SA keys from the table.

Use the **`vpn tu`** command to remove site-to-site IKE and/or IPSec keys and initiate traffic across the tunnel. This should place useful information into **`ike.elg`**. In the new **`ike.elg`** file, if you can identify on which packet the IKE negotiation fails, you can check relevant configuration parameters and correct accordingly. Also, look at the **`vpnd.elg`** file. This file contains useful information about other errors that might have occurred on the VPN tunnel establishment process.

# *VPN Debug*

## vpn debug

The command **vpn debug** contains multiple utilities for troubleshooting VPN issues. The following lists all options for the command:

```
vpn debug < on [ DEBUG_TOPIC=level ] | off | ikeon [
- s size(Mb) ]| ikeoff | trunc | truncon | truncoff
| timeon [ SECONDS ] | timeoff | ikefail [ -s
size(Mb) ]| mon | moff >
```

Run **-help** on the command to see a description of all the parameters. Below, you can find details on some specific options of the vpn debug command.

## vpn debug on | off

**`vpn debug on`** — Turn on **`vpn debug`**, and write the output to the following file: `vpnd.elg`

**`vpn debug on [debug topic]=[debug level]`** sets the specified **`TDERROR`** topic to the specified level, without affecting any other debug settings. This may be used to turn specific topics on or off.

**`vpn debug on TDERROR_ALL_ALL=1,2,3,4,5`** turns on default VPN debugging, i.e., all **`TDERROR`** output and default VPN topics, without affecting any other debug settings.

**`vpn debug off`** — Disable **`vpn debug`**.

## vpn debug ikeon | ikeoff

**`vpn debug ikeon`** — Turn on `ike debug` and write the output to the following file: `ike.elg`

**`vpn debug ikeoff`** — Disable `ike debug`.

## vpn Log Files

The **`ike.elg`** file contains information about the negotiation process for IKE encryption. The **`vpnd.elg`** contains verbose information regarding the negotiation process and other encryption failures. VPN debug logging is enabled using the **`vpn debug on`** command. The output of the debugging commands writes to two different locations, depending on what is being debugged:

- IKE debugging is written to **`$FWDIR/log/ike.elg`**.
- VPN debugging is written to **`$FWDIR/log/vpnd.elg`**.

## vpn debug trunc

When the `vpn debug on` command runs, the output is written to `$FWDIR\log\vpnd.elg` file by default.

## VPN Environment Variables

Setting environment variables to enable logging should only be performed in circumstances where VPNs are failing. The following are the commands to enable the variables:

- Windows — set `VPN_DEBUG=1`
- Unix — set `VPN_DEBUG 1`

In previous versions, Check Point recommended setting the environment variables to enable VPN debugging. As of VPN-1 NGX, **`vpn debug on`** is the preferred method. Setting the environment variables is recommended as a method for debugging, only if there is a VPN tunnel failure.

## vpn

The **`vpn`** command displays and controls various aspects of a Gateway. The following table lists other options for the vpn command that can be useful when troubleshooting/debugging a VPN related issue:

| Command | Description |
|---|---|
| vpn crl_zap | Erases all CRLs (Certificate Revocation Lists) from cache |
| vpn crlview | Debugging tool for CRLs |
| vpn tunneltuil<br>vpn tu | Displays a list of options to manage a VPN tunnel session; **`vpn tu`** can be used to stop all VPN or individual tunnels. |
| vpn drv <on \| off \| stat> | Attaches the VPN driver to fw driver; setting vpn drv to off will tear down all existing VPN tunnels, so caution should be used with this command. When vpn drv is set to on, all VPN tunnels are renegotiated, beginning at IKE Phase 1. |
| vpn ver [-k] | Displays VPN version |
| vpn accel <on \| off \| stat [-l]> | Displays operations on VPN Accelerator Card |
| vpn compstat | Display compression/decompression statistics |
| vpn compreset | Resets compression/decompression statistics |
| vpn export_p12 | Tool to export p12 from Gateway Certificate |

TABLE 2: vpn Command Options

## vpn tu

The command `vpn tu` is short for `vpn tunnelutil`, and is useful for deleting IPSec or IKE SAs to a specific peer or user without interrupting other VPN activities.

## Comparing SAs

The following is a quick process to verify that you and a potential VPN partner are configured correctly:

1. Enable VPN debugging on both your site and your partner's site with vpn debug on trunc.
2. Use `vpn tunnelutil` (`vpn tu`) to remove all SAs for either the peer with which you are about to create the tunnel, or all tunnels.
3. Have your peer initiate the tunnel from its site to yours.
4. Use `vpn tunnelutil` (`vpn tu`) to remove all SAs for either the peer with which you are about to create the tunnel, or all tunnels.
5. Initiate the tunnel from your site to your peer.
6. Disable debugging on both sites.
7. Examine `ike.elg` and `vpnd.elg`, as they will now contain records of the SA sent by your gateway, as well as what was received from your partner site.

## Examples

You have several site-to-site VPN tunnels among Gateways.

You want to remove the IKE SAs for a particular peer, without interrupting the other VPNs. How do you do that?

Run `vpn tu` from the Gateway Command Line Interface, and select **delete all IPSec and IKE SAs for a given Peer (GW)** option.

## VPN Encryption Issues

A typical issue with encryption is when Quick mode packet 1 fails with error "No Proposal Chosen" from the peer. This failure is usually caused when a peer does not agree to the proposal fields, such as encryption strength or hash.
A Security Gateway agrees loosely to the proposal, when it is host or network-based. Third-party vendors sometimes only agree to these proposals with strict adherence to defined parameters.

Another common problem is when a Security Gateway proposes a supernetted network address as the VPN Domain to a Cisco Concentrator (or other vendor) in phase 2. The Cisco device only agrees to a VPN Domain that matches its network address and subnet mask. This issue is known as the **Largest possible subnet** problem. Here are some troubleshooting steps for this issue:

- Check the **Shared Tunnel** settings in the **Tunnel Management** section of the VPN community. Make sure both sides agree on either host based or subnet based.

  Interoperable devices do not support the Gateway to Gateway option.
- In GuiDbedit, change the following property to false.
  **ike_use_largest_possible_subnet**

  This will prevent Check Point from supernetting networks in the VPN domain. The subnets defined in the network object should be used.
- Check for multiple network objects in the VPN domain that overlap. For example, 10.1.1.1/24 and 10.0.0.0/8 are both in the VPN domain. It is possible that a packet sourced from 10.1.x.x will use 255.0.0.0 for the subnet in phase 2 instead of 255.255.255.0.
- In some cases, particularly when network overlaps exist in the VPN domain, it is still required to modify the `user.def` file. See SecureKnowledge solution **sk19243** and **sk30919** on Check Point's Web site:

  **`https://usercenter.checkpoint.com/support`**

## Example 1

Assume you have a site-to-site VPN between two Check Point Security Gateways. They are managed by their own Management Servers. You see a lot of IKE Phase 1 failures in SmartView Tracker. You run IKE debug on one Gateway and discover only one packet in Main mode is transferred. There is no packet in Main mode after packet 1. What might have caused this problem?

First, check VPN settings (including Encryption Algorithm, key length, and Hash method) in the Community object. Make sure Phase 1 settings are identical on both sides. Also check Phase 1 settings in the Advanced settings in the Community object, such as group 1 or group 2, aggressive mode, etc. They must be defined identically on both sides.

## Example 2

You are configuring a site-to-site VPN from a Check Point Security Gateway to a Cisco device. You see that traffic initiated from the VPN Domain inside the Security Gateway is dropped with the error, “Packet is dropped as there is no valid SA”. The Cisco side is sending “Delete SA” to the Security Gateway. The IKE debug indicates a Phase 2 (Quick mode) failure. What is causing the misconfiguration?

A Quick mode failure usually indicates the VPN Domain is not configured exactly the same for one or both peers. For example, if the Security Gateway’s VPN Domain is a Class B network, but the same network is defined with a Class C subnet mask on the Cisco VPN configuration, then this type of error occurs.

# *Practice and Review*

## Practice Labs

Lab 5: Configuring Site-to-Site VPNs with Third Party Certificates

Lab 6: Remote Access with Endpoint Security VPN

## Review Questions

1. What are the stages of a Phase 2 IKE exchange?

2. What is the advantage of Link Selection for VPN traffic?

3. What type of VPN communities can be explicitly defined as MEP VPNs?

4. Quick mode packet 1 fails with error "No Proposal Chosen" from the peer. What is likely the cause?

CHAPTER 6

# *Auditing and Reporting*

# *Auditing and Reporting*

The SmartEvent Software Blade turns security information into action with real-time security event correlation and management for Check Point security gateways and third-party devices. SmartEvent's unified event analysis identifies critical security events from the clutter, while correlating events across all security systems. Its automated aggregation and correlation of data not only minimizes the time spent analyzing log data, but also isolates and prioritizes the real security threats.

The SmartReporter Software Blade centralizes reporting on network, security, and user activity and consolidates the data into concise predefined and custom-built reports. Easy report generation and automatic distribution save time and money.

## Objectives

- Create Events or use existing event definitions to generate reports on specific network traffic using SmartReporter and SmartEvent in order to provide industry compliance information to management.
- Using your knowledge of SmartEvent architecture and module communication, troubleshoot report generation given command-line tools and debug-file information.

# Auditing and Reporting Processes

From the standpoint of a network or security administrator, their role is completely guided by processes and procedures, and the need to document any changes implemented on the corporate network. In order to be compliant with industry standards, and corporate mandates, this documentation is a crucial part of an administrator's job.

Corporate governance, and the importance of efficient auditing and reporting, which takes place throughout the lifecycle of compliance regulatory practices is important.

## Auditing and Reporting Standards

The Sarbanes-Oxley Act of 2002 outlines **nine audit policies** for IT compliance checking. They ensure suspicious activity and system breaches are kept in-check by alerting corporate officials of potential threats. They include:

- Account logon
- Logon
- Account Management
- Policy Change
- Process Tracking
- Object Access
- Privilege Use
- System Events
- Directory Service Access

Implementing these audit policies produces detailed records for the following IT security aspects according to the Sarbanes-Oxley Act.

- Password changes
- Changes to access rights to shares, files, folders, etc.
- Attempts of unauthorized access to computer system resources
- Attempts of unauthorized access to information held in application systems
- All internal system activity, including logins, file accesses, and security incidents
- Produce and retain logs recording exceptions and security-related events
- Any attempts of unauthorized changes to IT systems
- Unauthorized changes to key system files and critical data
- Changes to Active Directory permissions for user accounts, groups and computer accounts
- Unauthorized Active Directory access permissions
- Any changes to users, groups, rights, and user account policies
- Notifications of group policy changes
- Authorized users attempts to perform unauthorized activities
- Permission changes in Active Directory
- User information, access information, date and time stamp
- Real-time policy modifications
- Last accessed dates for files and applications

Check Point's reporting tools generate thousands of events which include detailed log information. The automated processes in SmartEvent and SmartReporter provides a way to ease the workload of filtering all this raw material, to come up with a concise breakdown of meaningful data.

# SmartEvent

The Check Point SmartEvent Software Blade is a unified security event management and analysis solution that delivers real-time, actionable threat management information. Administrators can quickly identify critical security events, stop threats directly from the event screen, and add protections on-the-fly to remediate attacks, all via a single console..

Figure 33 — SmartEvent

The full SmartEvent Software Blade can monitor events for all Check Point products and third party devices. It includes pre-defined queries and event definitions for firewall, VPN, Endpoint Security, IPS, DLP, Identity Awareness and Application Control.

SmartEvent is available as a software blade or an appliance. The following management software blades are bundled in each SmartEvent appliance:

- SmartEvent
- SmartReporter
- Logging and Status

As part of the Software Blade architecture, the original Eventia Analyzer product name was changed to Event Correlation Software Blade. The Eventia Correlation Software Blade is renamed to SmartEvent Software Blade to better represent the product's unique value proposition.

## SmartEvent Intro

The SmartEvent Intro Software Blade provides centralized, real-time, security event correlation and management for a single Check Point Security Software Blade. For example, you could purchase the SmartEvent Intro Software Blade for either IPS or DLP event management.

The full reporting capabilities are a part of the SmartReporter Software Blade (which is bundled with the full SmartEvent Software Blade). It is possible to upgrade to the full SmartEvent version for full reporting. However, it is only possible to install one SmartEvent Intro Software Blade per device. To obtain monitoring and correlating firewall events, you would need the full SmartEvent Software Blade.

# SmartEvent Architecture

Three main components are responsible for producing the log consolidation, correlation and analysis results:

- **Correlation Unit (CU)** — Analyzes logs looking for patterns according to the installed Event Policy. When a threat pattern is identified, the CU forwards an event to the Eventia Analyzer Server.
- **Analyzer Server** — Receives events from the CU and assigns a severity level to the event. It invokes any defined automatic reactions, and adds the event to the Events Database, which resides here. The severity level and automatic reaction are based on the Events Policy. In addition, it imports certain objects from the management server to define the internal network. Changes made to the objects on the management server are reflected in the client. The Analyzer Server defines automatic responses and manages the database.
- **Analyzer Client** — The Windows GUI that displays the received events, and manages them for filtering and status (i.e., closed events). It provides fine-tuning and installation of the Events Policy.

An example of how the deployment scenario might look in an enterprise environment is the following:

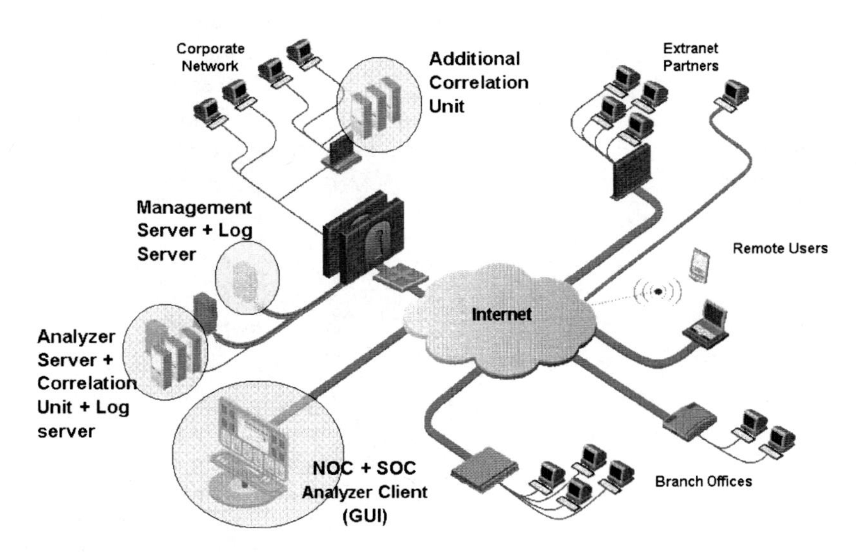


Figure 34 — Enterprise Environment

## Component Communication Process

Before going into any depth about how SmartEvent processes work, note the following different Check Point protocols, all of which are utilized here.

| Protocol | Type | Description |
|---|---|---|
| LEA | OPSEC | Log Export API |
| ELA | OPSEC | Event Logging API |
| SAM | OPSEC | Suspicious Activity Monitoring |
| AMON | OPSEC | Application Monitoring |
| CPMI | OPSEC | Check Point Management Interface to access Check Point object database objects |
| CPLOG | Internal | Like ELA, but is based on local communication |
| FWM Command | Internal | RPC infrastructure to send commands such as: database queries, data-cube requests |
| Guaranteed Delivery | Internal | Passes events from Correlation Unit to the Analyzer Server |
| CPTA | Internal | Event policy Installation |
| Dbsync | Internal | Uses CPMI |

Figure 35 — SmartEvent Processes

Referring to the next graphic, note that the Analyzer Server provides the event definitions by way of the Event Policy to the CU, which in turn, pulls the logs originating from the log sources, i.e., third party log servers. The CU performs its analysis based on the Event Policy and delivers the results to the Server. The Server communicates this information to the client.

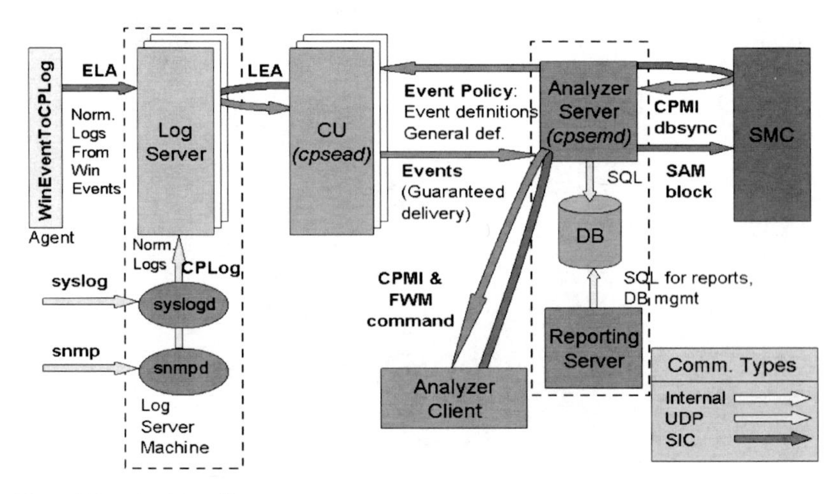


Figure 36 — Analyzer Server

## Event Policy User Interface

As you can see, the Event Policy is fundamental to the workings of SmartEvent, and deserves a closer look. In this section, we'll look at how to edit event properties in order to customize or tailor events to your organization.

To open a properties window, from the **Policy** tab, right-click on an event, and from the drop-down box, select **Properties**.

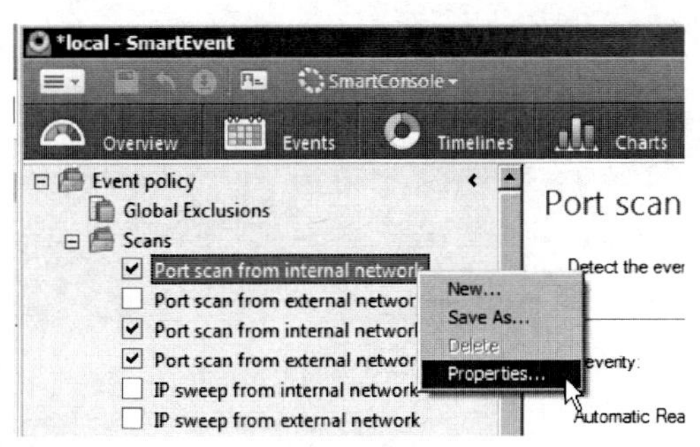


Figure 37 — SmartEvent Policy

This opens the main Edit Event Definition window. There are five tabs used to configure the event.

We'll be paying close attention to the **Filter** tab.

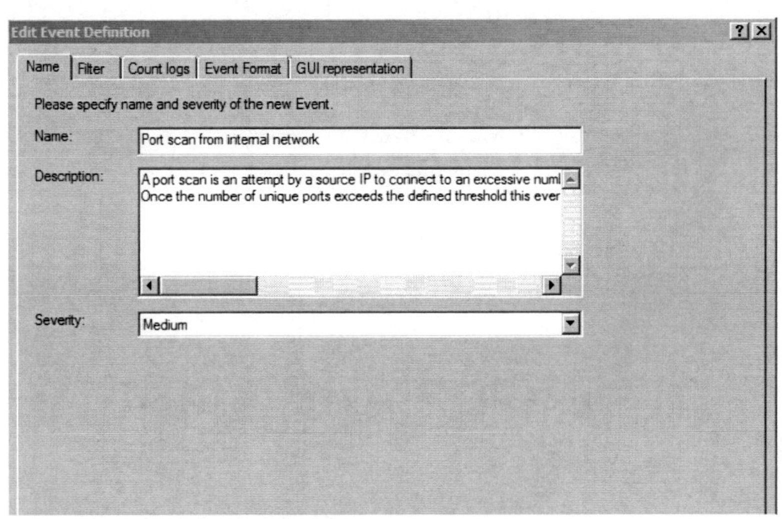


Figure 38 — Edit Event Definition

The filter tab settings determine whether a log is considered for an event or not. Events that don't match the defined filters are discarded.

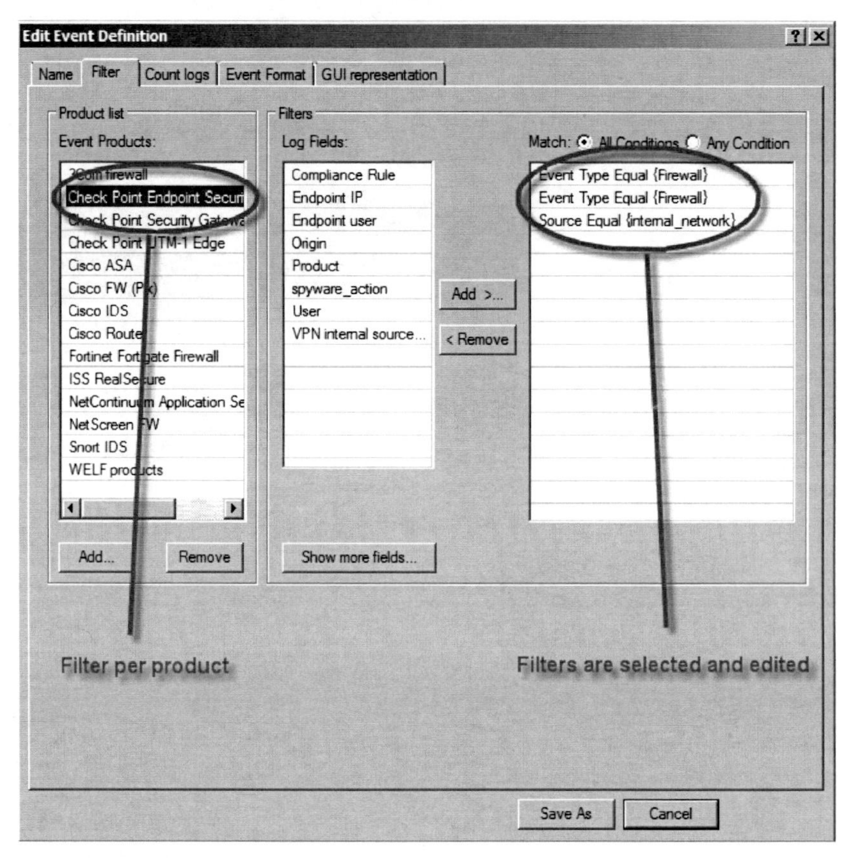


Figure 39 — Edit Event Definition

In the **Count Logs** tab, you define the number of logs collected over a period of time that determines a new event.

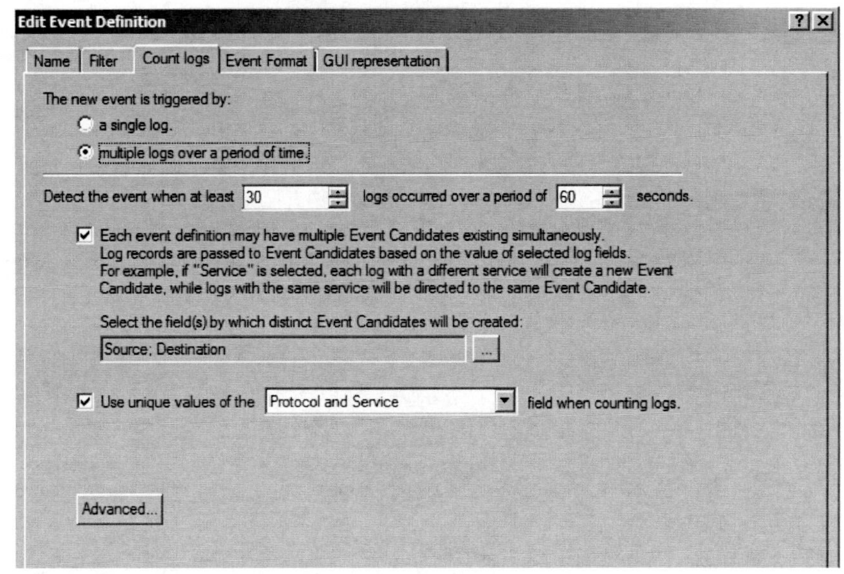


Figure 40 — Edit Event Definition

When clicking on the **Advanced** button from here, you can decide to keep an event open (i.e., Time to live), which means that after an event is generated, more logs are accumulated to the event until the event falls below the threshold time.

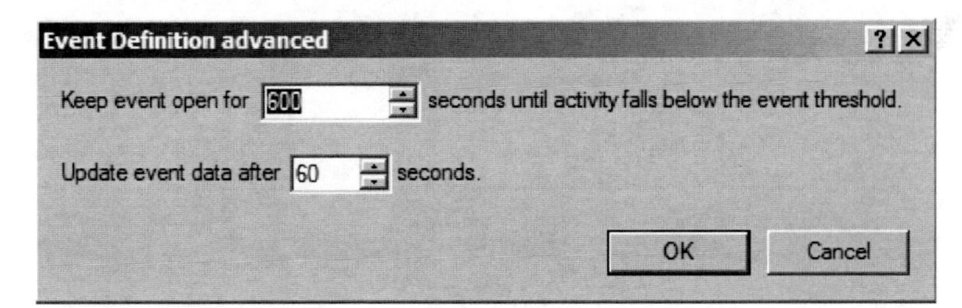


Figure 41 — Event Definition Advanced

The Updated time means an event is updated after the designated length of time. Actually, the event is reported several times:

- When created
- Up to five updates
- When it is closed

The **Event Format** tab permits mapping Event data to log fields so that the actual Event is viewed with the corresponding (preferential) data.

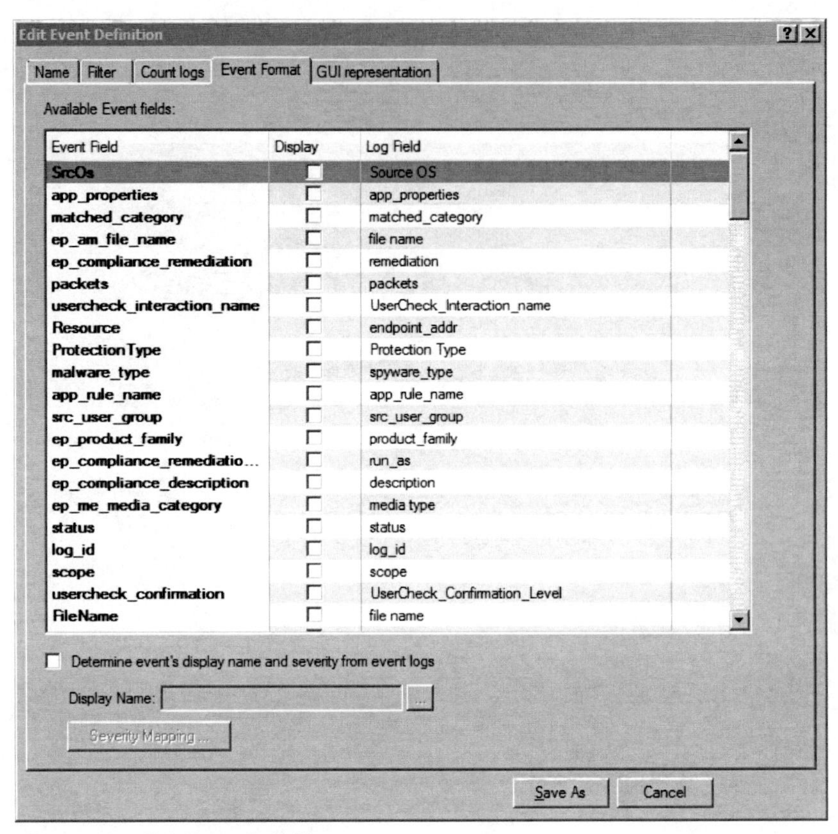


Figure 42 — Edit Event Definition

Finally, the GUI representation tab allows the administrator to define which fields (and how wide the field) will display in the exception and exclusion sections of the particular event policy.

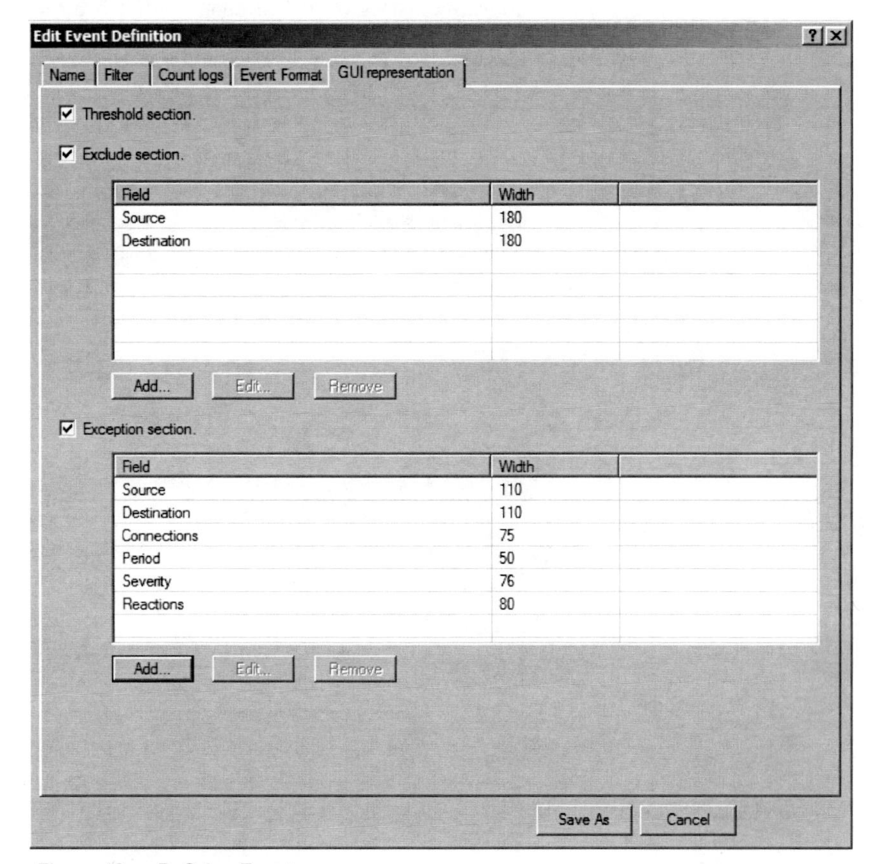


Figure 43 — Defining Events

When creating a new event, from the Event Definition Wizard, you can select an event as the basis for the new event, or create a new event from scratch. If you used the Save As option from the drop-down menu you saw earlier, you can clone an existing event and then modify it for a new event.

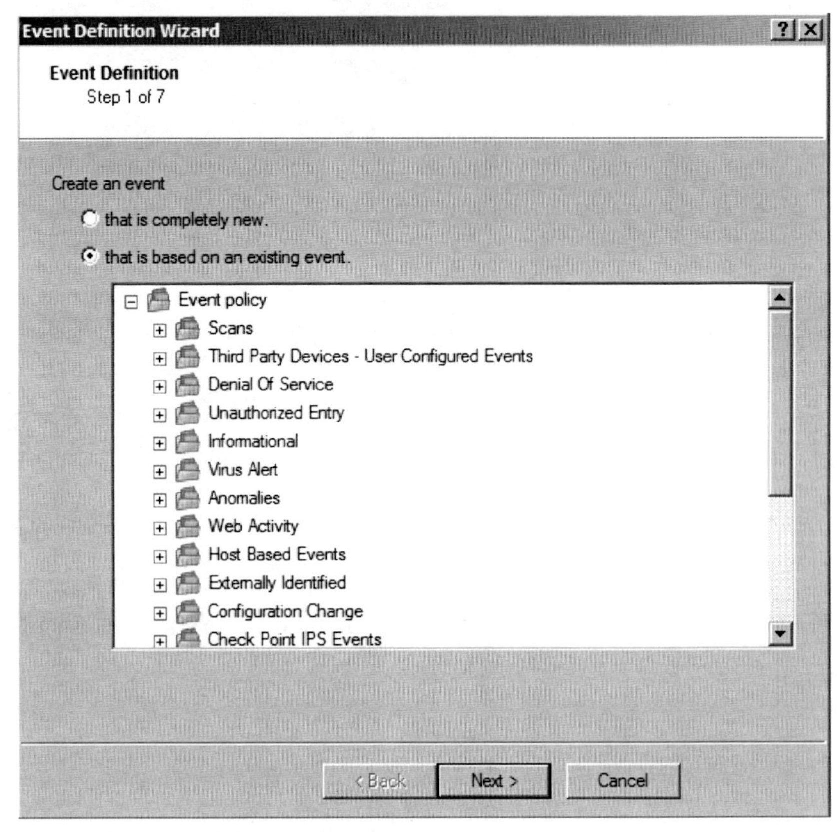


Figure 44 — Event Definition Wizard - Step 1

The wizard will guide you through setting up the basics of the event, such as name and description. In addition, you can decide if an event will be generated by a single log that matches the event definition, or multiple logs. When making this choice, ask yourself, "Is the receipt of a single log, enough to imply an event?"

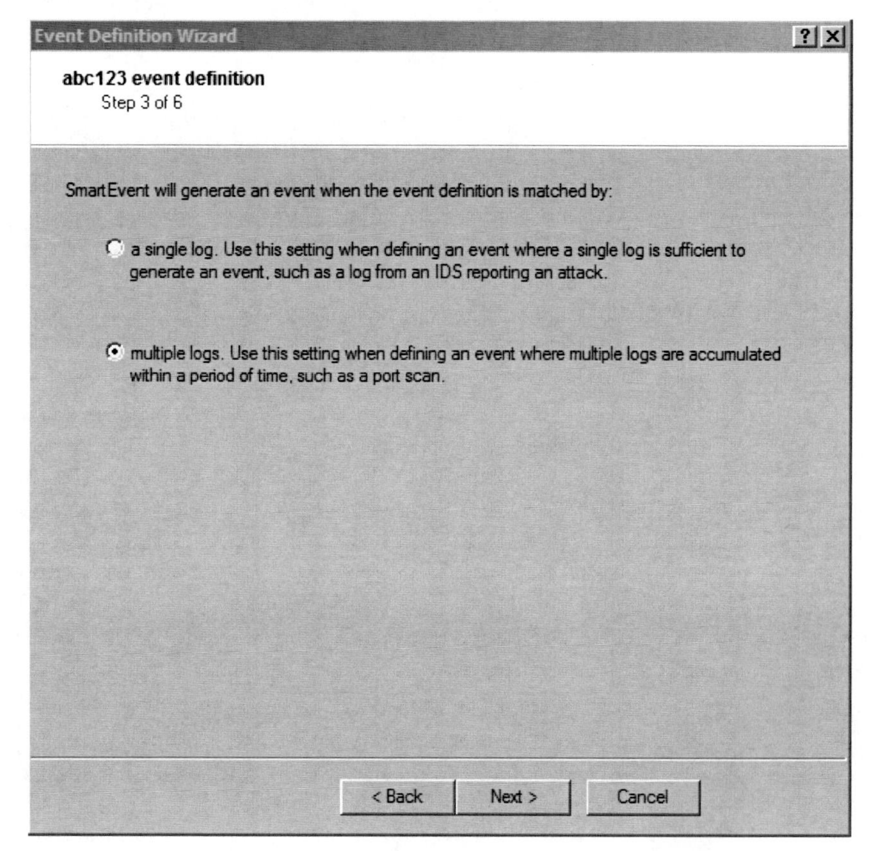


Figure 45 — Event Definition Wizard - Step 3

The next step in the wizard guides you in building the filter. You start by designating the source product, then choosing among the available log fields as a condition for the match.

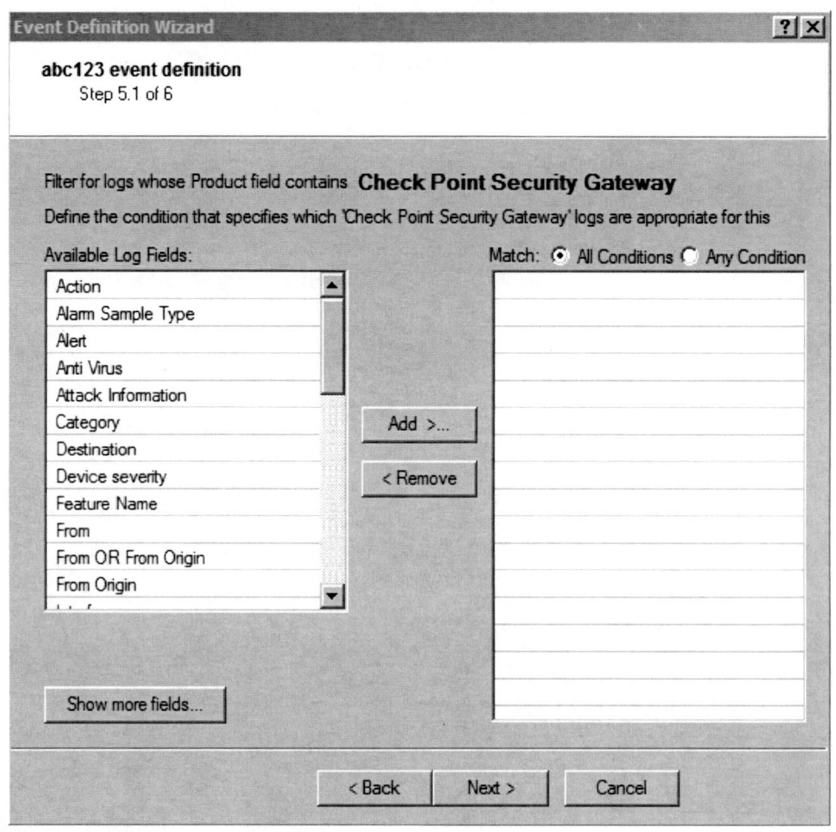

Figure 46 — Event Definition Wizard - Action Filter

Finally, you specify the threshold, time, distinct values and unique values:

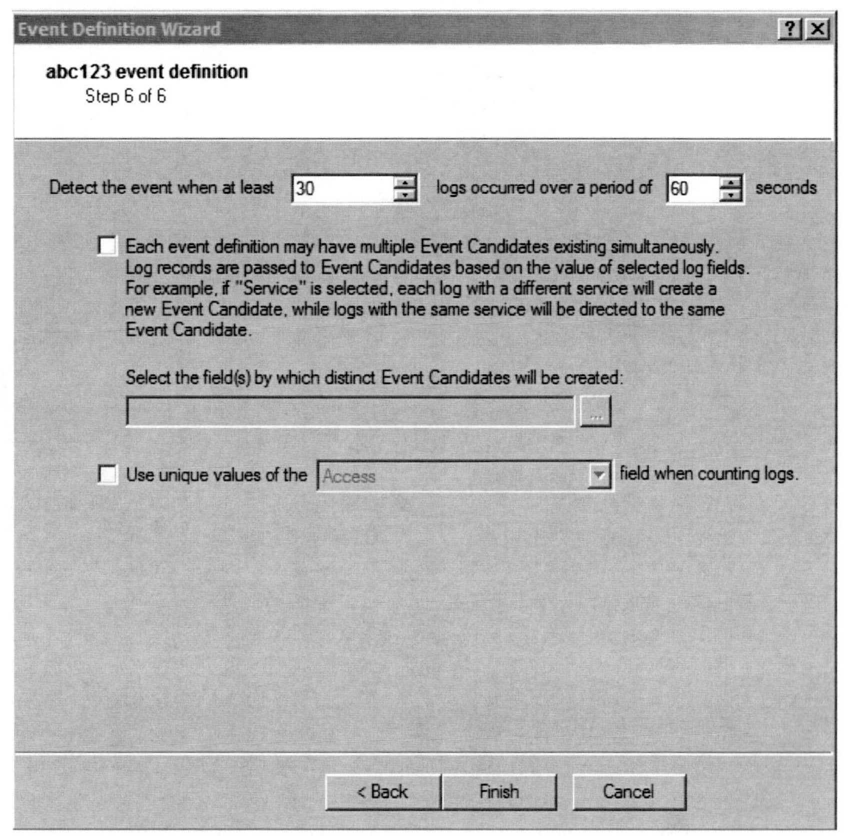


Figure 47 — Event Definition Wizard - Step 6

Clicking **Finish** will save the new event under the list of **User Defined Events**. In order for it to take effect however, you must remember to install the event policy from the **Actions** menu, option **Install Event policy**.

# SmartReporter

The purpose of SmartReporter is to provide an understanding of important events (traffic) occurring on the network, and the overall security impact of those events. It provides:

- High-level view, trends, reports
- Understanding of the details of each event
- Integration with other tools to modify the security policies
- Manage events by state and owner

SmartReporter implements a Consolidation Policy, which goes over your original, "raw" log file. It compresses similar events and writes the compressed list of events into a relational database (the SmartReporter Database). This database enables quick and efficient generation of a wide range of reports.

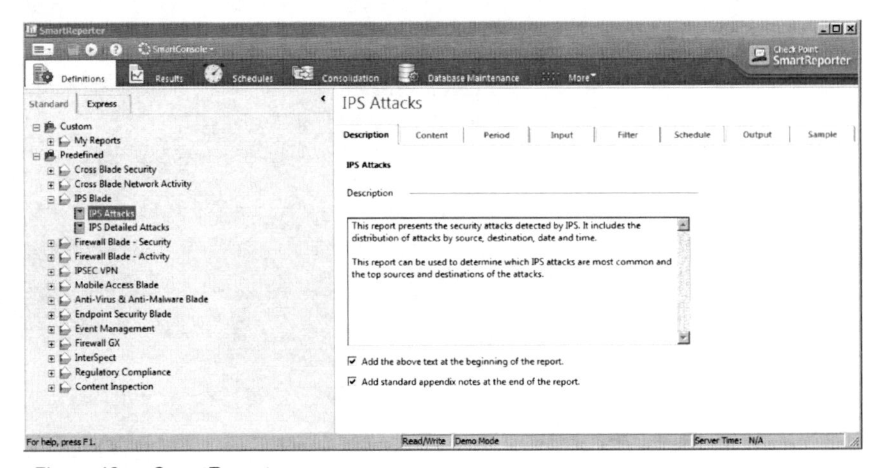


Figure 48 — SmartReporter

A Consolidation Policy is similar to a Security Policy in terms of its structure and management. For example, both Rule Bases are defined through the SmartDashboard's Rules menu and use the same network objects. In addition, just as Security Rules determine whether to allow or deny the connections that match them, Consolidation Rules determine whether to store or ignore the logs that match them. The key difference is that a Consolidation Policy is based on logs, as opposed to connections, and has no bearing on security issues.

The Log Consolidation Solution diagram illustrates the Consolidation process, defined by the Consolidation Policy.

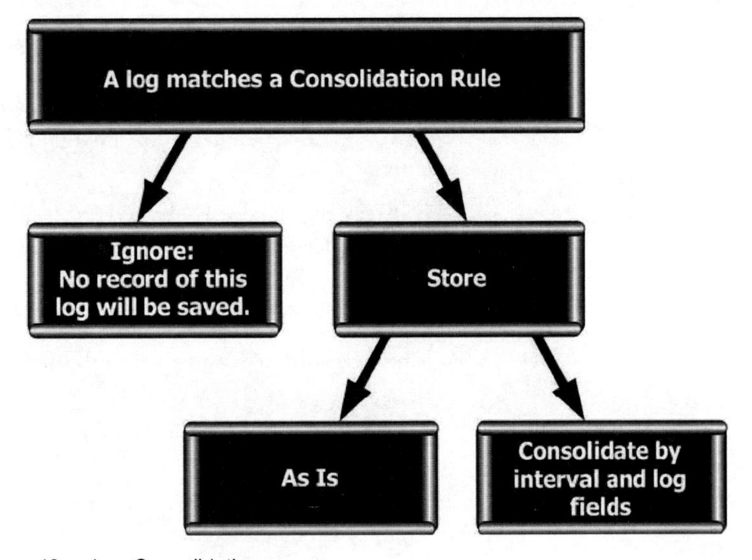


Figure 49 — Log Consolidation

After the Security Gateways send their logs to the Security Management server, the Log Consolidator Engine collects them, scans them, filters out fields defined as irrelevant, merges records defined as similar and saves them to the SmartReporter Database.

The Figure illustrates how the Consolidation Policy processes logs: when a log matches a Consolidation Rule, it is either ignored or stored. If it is ignored, no record of this log is saved in the SmartReporter system, so its data is not available for report generation. If it is stored, it is either saved as is (so all log fields can later be represented in reports), or consolidated to the level specified by the Rule.

The consolidation is performed on two levels: the interval at which the log was created, and the log fields whose original values should be retained. When several logs matching a specific Rule are recorded within a predefined interval, the values of their relevant fields are saved "as is", while the values of their irrelevant fields are merged (for example, "consolidated") together.

The SmartReporter server can then extract the consolidated records matching a specific report definition from the SmartReporter Database and present them in a report layout.

## Report Types

Two types of reports can be created:

- **Standard Reports** — The Standard Reports are generated from information in log files through the Consolidation process to yield relevant analysis of activity.
- **Express Reports** — Express Reports are generated from SmartView Monitor History files and are produced much more quickly.

SmartReporter Standard Reports are supported by two Clients:

- **SmartDashboard Log Consolidator** — manages the Log Consolidation rules.
- **SmartReporter Client** — generates and manages reports.

The interaction between the SmartReporter client and Server components applies both to a distributed installation, where the Security Management server and SmartReporter's Server components are installed on two different machines, and to a standalone installation, in which these Software Blades are installed on the same machine.

# Practice and Review

## Practice Lab

Lab 7: SmartEvent and SmartReporter

## Review Questions

1. What does the SmartReporter Consolidation Policy do?

2. What is the difference between a Consolidation Policy, and a Security Policy?

3. When is an event reported?

Appendix A

# *Gaia Maintenance*

## Licenses

Licenses can be added or deleted using the:

- Maintenance > Licenses page of the WebUI
- Command line by running: cplic db_add or cplic del.

**Note:** While all the SecurePlatform cplic commands are available in Gaia, they are not grouped into a Gaia feature. To see a list of available commands and their parameters type cplic and press Enter.

## Configuring Licenses - WebUI

If you need to obtain a license, visit the User Center.

### *Adding a license:*

1. In the tree view, click Maintenance > Licenses.
2. Click New.

   The Add License window opens.
3. Enter the license data manually, or click Paste License to enter the data automatically.

   The Paste License button only shows in Internet Explorer. For other browsers, paste the license strings into the empty text field.

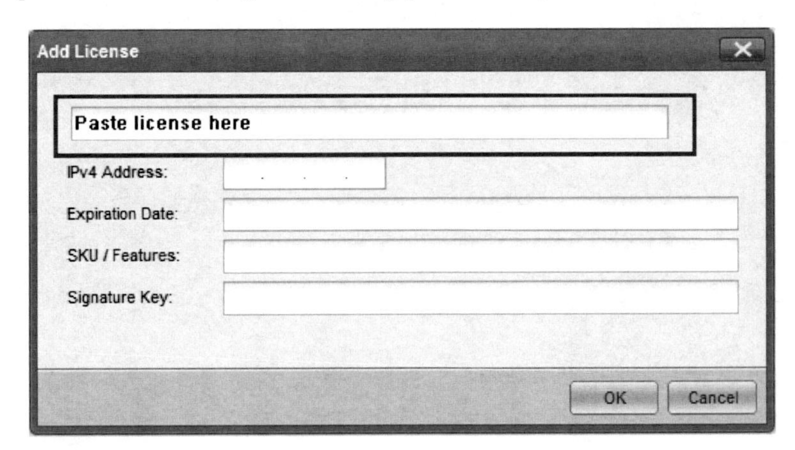


4. Click OK.

### *Deleting a license:*

1. In the tree view, click Maintenance > Licenses.
2. Select a license in the table
3. Click Delete.

## Configuring Licenses - CLI (cplic)

The cplic command and all its derivatives relate to Check Point license management.

> **Note:** The SmartUpdate GUI is the recommended way of managing licenses.

All cplic commands are located in $CPDIR/bin. License Management is divided into three types of commands:

- Local licensing commands are executed on local machines.
- Remote licensing commands are commands which affect remote machines are executed on the Security Management server.
- License repository commands are executed on the Security Management server.

### *Syntax*

Local Licensing:

```
 cplic put ...
cplic del [-F <output file>] <signature>
cplic print [-h help] [-n noheader]
            [-x print signatures] [-t type]
            [-F <output file>] [-i <input file>]
            [-p preatures]
            [-D print only Domain licenses]
cplic check ...
cplic contract ...
```

Remote Licensing:

```
 cplic put <object name> ...
cplic del <object name> [-F <output file>] <signature>
cplic get <object name | -all>
```

```
cplic upgrade -l input file
```

License Database Operations:

```
cplic db_add ...
cplic db_rm <signature>
cplic db_print <object name | -all> ...
```

For help on any command add the -h option

## cplic check

Description: Check whether the license on the local machine will allow a given feature to be used.

Usage: cplic check [-p <product name>] [-v <product version>] [-c count] [-t <date>] [-r routers] [-S SRusers] <feature>

Syntax:

| Argument | Description |
|---|---|
| -p <product name> | Product for which license information is requested. For example fw1, netso |
| -v <product version> | Product version for which license information is requested |
| -c count | Output the number of licenses connected to this feature |
| -t <date> | Check license status on future date. Use the format ddmmmyyyy. A feature may be valid on a given date on one license, but invalid in another |
| -r routers | Check how many routers are allowed. The feature option is not needed |
| -S SRusers | Check how many SecuRemote users are allowed. The feature option is not needed |
| <feature> | <feature> for which license information is requested |

TABLE 3: cplic check

## cplic db_add

Description: Used to add one or more licenses to the license repository on the Security Management server. When local license are added to the license repository, they are automatically attached to its intended Check Point gateway, central licenses need to undergo the attachment process.

This command is a license repository command, it can only be executed on the Security Management server.

Usage: cplic db_add < -l license-file | host expiration-date signature SKU/ features >

Syntax:

| Argument | Description |
|---|---|
| -l license-file | Adds the license(s) from license-file. The following options are NOT needed:<br>Host Expiration-Date Signature SKU/feature |

TABLE 4: cplic db_add

Comments: Copy/paste the following parameters from the license received from the User Center. More than one license can be added.

- **host** — the target hostname or IP address.
- **expiration date** — The license expiration date.
- **signature** —The License signature string. For example: aa6uwknDc-CE6CRtjhv-zipoVWSnm-z98N7Ck3m (Case sensitive. The hyphens are optional.)
- **SKU/features** — The SKU of the license summarizes the features included in the license. For example: CPSUITE-EVAL-3DES-vNG

Example: If the file 192.0.2.11.lic contains one or more licenses, the command: cplic db_add -l 192.0.2.11.lic will produce output similar to the following:

```
Adding license to database ...

Operation Done
```

## cplic db_print

Description: Displays the details of Check Point licenses stored in the license repository on the Security Management server.

Usage: cplic db_print <object name | -all> [-n noheader] [-x print signatures] [-t type] [-a attached]

Syntax:

| Argument | Description |
|---|---|
| Object name | Print only the licenses attached to Object name. Object name is the name of the Check Point Security Gateway object, as defined in SmartDashboard. |
| -all | Print all the licenses in the license repository |
| -noheader<br>(or -n) | Print licenses with no header. |
| -x | Print licenses with their signature |
| -t<br>(or -type) | Print licenses with their type: Central or Local. |
| -a<br>(or -attached) | Show which object the license is attached to. Useful if the -all option is specified. |

TABLE 5: cplic db_print

Comments: This command is a license repository command, it can only be executed on the Security Management server.

## cplic db_rm

Description: The cplic db_rm command removes a license from the license repository on the Security Management server. It can be executed ONLY after the license was detached using the cplic del command. Once the license has been removed from the repository, it can no longer be used.

Usage: cplic db_rm <signature>

Syntax:

| Argument | Description |
| --- | --- |
| Signature | The signature string within the license. |

TABLE 6: cplic db_rm

Example: cplic db_rm 2f540abb-d3bcb001-7e54513e-kfyigpwn

Comments:This command is a license repository command, it can only be executed on the Security Management server.

## cplic del

Description: Delete a single Check Point license on a host, including unwanted evaluation, expired, and other licenses. Used for both local and remote machines

Usage: cplic del [-F <output file>] <signature> <object name>

Syntax:

| Argument | Description |
| --- | --- |
| -F <output file> | Send the output to <output file> instead of the screen. |
| <signature> | The signature string within the license. |

TABLE 7: cplic del

## cplic del <object name>

Description: Detach a Central license from a Check Point gateway. When this command is executed, the license repository is automatically updated. The Central license remains in the repository as an unattached license. This command can be executed only on a Security Management server.

Usage: cplic del <Object name> [-F outputfile] [-ip dynamic ip] <Signature>

Syntax:

| Argument | Description |
|---|---|
| object name | The name of the Check Point Security Gateway object, as defined in SmartDashboard. |
| -F outputfile | Divert the output to outputfile rather than to the screen |
| -ip dynamic ip | Delete the license on the Check Point Security Gateway with the specified IP address. This parameter is used for deleting a license on a DAIP Check Point Security Gateway<br>Note - If this parameter is used, then object name must be a DAIP gateway. |
| Signature | The signature string within the license. |

TABLE 8: cplic del <object name>

Comments: This is a Remote Licensing Command which affects remote machines that is executed on the Security Management server.

## cplic get

Description: The cplic get command retrieves all licenses from a Check Point Security Gateway (or from all Check Point gateways) into the license repository on the Security Management server. Do this to synchronize the repository with the Check Point gateway(s). When the command is run, all local changes will be updated.

Usage: cplic get <ipaddr | hostname | -all> [-v41]

Syntax:

| Argument | Description |
|---|---|
| ipaddr | The IP address of the Check Point Security Gateway from which licenses are to be retrieved. |
| hostname | The name of the Check Point Security Gateway object (as defined in SmartDashboard) from which licenses are to be retrieved. |
| -all | Retrieve licenses from all Check Point gateways in the managed network. |
| -v41 | Retrieve version 4.1 licenses from the NF Check Point gateway. Used to upgrade version 4.1 licenses. |

TABLE 9: cplic get

Example: If the Check Point Security Gateway with the object name caruso contains four Local licenses, and the license repository contains two other Local licenses, the command: cplic get caruso produces output similar to the following:

```
Get retrieved 4 licenses.
Get removed 2 licenses.
```

Comments: This is a Remote Licensing Command which affects remote machines that is executed on the Security Management server.

## cplic put

Description: Install one or more Local licenses on a local machine.

Usage: cplic put [-o overwrite] [-c check-only] [-s select] [-F <output file>]

[-P Pre-boot] [-k kernel-only] <-l license-file | host expiration date signature SKU/feature>

Syntax:

| Argument | Description |
|---|---|
| -overwrite<br>(or -o) | On a Security Management server this will erase all existing licenses and replace them with the new license(s). On a Check Point Security Gateway this will erase only Local licenses but not Central licenses, that are installed remotely |
| -check-only<br>(or -c) | Verify the license. Checks if the IP of the license matches the machine, and if the signature is valid |
| select<br>(or -s) | Select only the Local licenses whose IP address matches the IP address of the machine. |
| -F outputfile | Outputs the result of the command to the designated file rather than to the screen. |
| -Preboot<br>(or -P) | Use this option after upgrading and before rebooting the machine. Use of this option will prevent certain error messages. |
| -kernel-only<br>(or -k) | Push the current valid licenses to the kernel. For Support use only. |
| -l license-file | Installs the license(s) in license-file, which can be a multi-license file. The following options are NOT needed:<br>host expiration-date signature SKU/features |

TABLE 10: cplic put

Comments: Copy and paste the following parameters from the license received from the User Center.

- **host** — One of the following:

  - All platforms - The IP address of the external interface (in dot notation); last part cannot be 0 or 255.
- **expiration date** — The license expiration date. Can be never.
- **signature** —The License signature string. For example: aa6uwknDc-CE6CRtjhv-zipoVWSnm-z98N7Ck3m (Case sensitive. The hyphens are optional.)

- **SKU/features** — A string listing the SKU and the Certificate Key of the license. The SKU of the license summarizes the features included in the license. For example: CPMP-EVAL-1-3DES-NG CK0123456789ab

Example: cplic put -l 215.153.142.130.lic produces output similar to the following:

```
Host             Expiration  SKU
215.153.142.130  26Dec2001   CPMP-EVAL-1-3DES-NG CK0123456789ab
```

## cplic put <object name> ...

Description: Use the cplic put command to attach one or more central or local license remotely. When this command is executed, the license repository is also updated.

Usage: cplic put <object name> [-ip dynamic ip] [-F <output file>] < -l license-file | host expiration-date signature SKU/features >

Syntax:

| Argument | Description |
|---|---|
| object name | The name of the Check Point Security Gateway object, as defined in SmartDashboard. |
| -ip dynamic ip | Install the license on the Check Point Security Gateway with the specified IP address. This parameter is used for installing a license on a DAIP Check Point gateway.<br><br>NOTE: If this parameter is used, then object name must be a DAIP Check Point gateway. |
| -F outputfile | Divert the output to outputfile rather than to the screen |
| -l license-file | Installs the license(s) from license-file. The following options are NOT needed:<br><br>Host Expiration-Date Signature SKU/features |

TABLE 11: cplic put <object name>

Comments: This is a Remote Licensing Command which affects remote machines that is executed on the Security Management server.

Copy and paste the following parameters from the license received from the User Center. More than one license can be attached.

- **host** — the target hostname or IP address.
- **expiration date** — The license expiration date. Can be never.
- **signature** —The License signature string. For example: aa6uwknDc-CE6CRtjhv-zipoVWSnm-z98N7Ck3m (Case sensitive. The hyphens are optional)
- **SKU/features** — A string listing the SKU and the Certificate Key of the license. The SKU of the license summarizes the features included in the license. For example: CPMP-EVAL-1-3DES-NG CK0123456789ab

## cplic print

Description: The cplic print command (located in $CPDIR/bin) prints details of Check Point licenses on the local machine.

Usage: cplic print [-n noheader][-x prints signatures][-t type][-F <outputfile>] [-p preatures]

Syntax:

| Argument | Description |
|---|---|
| -noheader<br>(or -n) | Print licenses with no header. |
| -x | Print licenses with their signature |
| -type<br>(or -t) | Prints licenses showing their type: Central or Local. |
| -F <outputfile> | Divert the output to outputfile. |
| -preatures<br>(or -p) | Print licenses resolved to primitive features. |

TABLE 12: cplic print

Comments: On a Check Point gateway, this command will print all licenses that are installed on the local machine — both Local and Central licenses.

## cplic upgrade

Description: Use the cplic upgrade command to upgrade licenses in the license repository using licenses in a license file obtained from the User Center.

Usage: cplic upgrade <–l inputfile>

Syntax:

| Argument | Description |
|---|---|
| –l inputfile | Upgrades the licenses in the license repository and Check Point gateways to match the licenses in <inputfile> |

TABLE 13: cplic upgrade

Example: The following example explains the procedure which needs to take place in order to upgrade the licenses in the license repository.

- Upgrade the Security Management server to the latest version.
- Ensure that there is connectivity between the Security Management server and the Security Gateways with the previous version products.
- Import all licenses into the license repository. This can also be done after upgrading the products on the remote gateways.
- Run the command: cplic get –all. For example:

```
Getting licenses from all modules ...


count:root(su) [~] # cplic get -all
golda:
Retrieved 1 licenses.
Detached  0 licenses.
Removed  0 licenses.
count:
Retrieved 1 licenses.
Detached  0 licenses.
Removed   0 licenses.
```

- To see all the licenses in the repository, run the command: cplic db_print -all –a

```
count:root(su) [~] # cplic db_print -all -a
Retrieving license information from database ...
The following licenses appear in the database:
==================================================

Host        Expiration Features
192.0.2.11  Never      CPFW-FIG-25-53          CK-49C3A3CC7121 golda
192.0.2.11  26Nov2012  CPSUITE-EVAL-3DES-NGX CK-1234567890   count
```

- In the User Center, view the licenses for the products that were upgraded from version NGX to a Software Blades license and create new upgraded licenses.
- Download a file containing the upgraded licenses. Only download licenses for the products that were upgraded from version NGX to Software Blades.
- If you did not import the version NGX licenses into the repository, import the version NGX licenses now using the command cplic get -all
- Run the license upgrade command: cplic upgrade –l <inputfile>

  - The licenses in the downloaded license file and in the license repository are compared.

  - If the certificate keys and features match, the old licenses in the repository and in the remote Security Gateways are updated with the new licenses.

  - A report of the results of the license upgrade is printed.
- In the example, there are two Software Blades licenses in the file. One does not match any license on a remote Security Gateway, the other matches a version NGX license on a Security Gateway that should be upgraded:

Comments: This is a Remote Licensing Command which affects remote Security Gateways, that is executed on the Security Management server.

Further Info. See the SmartUpdate chapter of the R76 Installation and Upgrade Guide.

## Image Management

You can:

- Make a new image (a snapshot) of the system. You can revert to the image at a later time.
- Revert to a locally stored image. This restores the system, including the configuration of the installed products.
- Delete an image from the local system.

- Export an existing image. This creates a compressed version of the image. You can then download the exported image to another computer and delete the exported image from the Gaia computer, to save disk space.
- Import uploads an exported image and makes an image of it (a snapshot). You can revert to the image at a later time.
- View a list of images that are stored locally.

## Configuring Image Management - WebUI

To create an image:

1. In the tree view, click Maintenance > Image Management.
2. Below available images, click New Image. The Create New Image window opens.
3. In the Name field, enter a name for the image.
4. Optional: In the Description field, enter a description for the image.
5. Click OK.

> **Note:** To create the snapshot requires free space on the Backup partition. The required free disk space is the actual size of the root partition, multiplied by 1.15.

To revert to an image:

1. In the tree view, click Maintenance > Image Management.
2. Select an image.
3. Click Revert. The Revert window opens.

   > **Note:** Pay close attention to the warnings about overwriting settings, the credentials, and the reboot and the image details.

4. Click OK.

To delete an image:

1. In the tree view, click Maintenance > Image Management.
2. Select an image.
3. Click Delete. The Delete Image window opens.
4. Click Ok.

To export an image:

1. In the tree view, click Maintenance > Image Management.

2. Select an image.
3. Click Export. The Export Image (name) window.
4. Click Start Export.

**Note:** The snapshot image exports to /var/log. The free space required in the export file storage location is the size of the snapshot multiplied by two.
The minimum size of a snapshot is 2.5G, so the minimum free space you need in the export file storage location is 5G.

To import an image:

1. In the tree view, click Maintenance > Image Management.
2. Select an image.
3. Click Import. The Import Image window opens.
4. Click Browse to select the import file for upload.
5. Click Upload.
6. Click OK.

## Configuring Image Management - CLI (snapshot)

Description: Manage system images (also known as snapshots)

Syntax:

To make a new image:

```
add snapshot VALUE desc VALUE
```

To delete an image

```
delete snapshot VALUE
```

To export or import an image, or to revert to an image:

```
set snapshot export VALUE path VALUE name VALUE
set snapshot import VALUE path VALUE name VALUE
set snapshot revert VALUE
```

To show image information

```
show snapshot VALUE all
show snapshot VALUE date
```

```
show snapshot VALUE desc
show snapshot VALUE size
show snapshots
```

Parameters:

| Parameter | Description |
|---|---|
| snapshot VALUE | Name of the image |
| desc VALUE | Description of the image |
| snapshot export VALUE | The name of the image to export |
| snapshot import VALUE | The name of the image to import |
| path VALUE | The storage location for the exported image. For example: /var/log |
| name VALUE | The name of the exported image (not the original image). |
| all | All image details |

TABLE 14: snapshot

Comments:

- To create the snapshot image requires free space on the Backup partition. The required free disk space is the actual size of the root partition, multiplied by 1.15.
- The free space required in the export file storage location is the size of the snapshot multiplied by two.
- The minimum size of a snapshot is 2.5G, so the minimum free space you need in the export file storage location is 5G.

## Download SmartConsole

You can download the SmartConsole application package from a Gaia Security Management server to your WebUI client computer. After downloading the package you can install it and use it to connect to the Security Management server.

## Download SmartConsole - WebUI

To download the Check Point SmartConsole applications installation package:

1. In the tree view, select one of:
    - Overview. At the top of the page, click Download Now!
    - Maintenance > Download SmartConsole.
2. Click Download.

## Hardware Health Monitoring

You can monitor these hardware elements:

- Fan sensors (shows the fan number, status, and value)
- System Temperature sensor
- Voltage sensors
- Power Supply (on machines that support it)

## Showing Hardware Health Monitoring Information - WebUI

In the navigation tree, click Maintenance > Hardware Health.

You can see the status of the machine fans, system temperature, the voltages, and (for supported hardware only) the power supply.

> **Note:** The Hardware Health Monitoring page only appears for supported hardware.

For each component sensor, the table shows the value of its operation, and the status: OK, Low, or High.

- To see the health history of a component, select the component sensor. A graph shows the values over time.
- To change the time intervals that the graph shows, click the Minute arrows.
- To view different times, click the Forward/Backward arrows.
- To refresh, click Refresh.

## Showing Hardware Monitoring Information - CLI (sysenv)

Description: These commands display the status for various system components. Components for which the status can be displayed include temperature, voltage, power supplies, and fans. The command returns status only for installed components.

Syntax: To display all system status information:

```
show sysenv all
```

To display all system component information:

```
show sysenv fans
show sysenv ps
show sysenv temp
show sysenv volt
```

Parameters:

| Parameter | Description |
|---|---|
| ps | Power Supply (for supported hardware only) |

TABLE 15: sysenv

Example: show sysenv all

Output:

```
gw-3002f0> show sysenv all

Hardware Information

Name    Value    unit     type      status  Maximum  Minimum
+12V    29.44    Volt     Voltage     0       12.6     11.4
+5V      6.02    Volt     Voltage     0       5.3      4.75
VBat     3.23    Volt     Voltage     0       3.47     2.7
```

## Showing Hardware Information - CLI (show asset)

Description: Shows information about the hardware on which Gaia is installed. The information shown depends on the type of hardware. Common types of information shown are:

- Serial number
- Amount of physical RAM
- CPU frequency
- Number of disks in the system
- Disk capacity

Syntax:

```
show asset all
show asset <TAB>
show asset <category name>
```

Parameters:

| Parameter | Description |
| --- | --- |
| all | Show all available hardware information. The information shown depends on the type of hardware. |
| <TAB> | Show a list of asset categories, such as system and disk. The available categories depend on the type of hardware. |
| <category name> | Show available information for a specific category |

TABLE 16: show asset

Example 1

```
clish> show asset
```

Output 1

```
system all
```

Example 2

```
clish> show asset all
```

Output 2

```
Platform: Check Point 4400
Serial Number: abcdefghijklmn
CPU Frequency: 2600Mhz
Disk Size: 250GB
```

## Shutdown

There are two ways to shut down:

- Reboot: Shut down the system and then immediately restart it.
- Halt: Shut down the system.

## Shutting Down - WebUI

To shut down the system and then immediately restart it:

1. In the tree view, click Maintenance > Shut Down.
2. Click Reboot.

To shut down the system:

1. In the tree view, click Maintenance > Shut Down.
2. Click Halt.

## Shutting Down - CLI (halt, reboot)

To shut down the system and then immediately restart it: Run the reboot command.

To shut down the system: Run the halt command.

## System Configuration Backup

This feature is available in a R75.40 Gaia Feature Release (Gaia+) clean installation. It is not available when upgrading to R75.40 Gaia.

- Back up the configuration of the Gaia operating system and of the Security Management server database. You can use the backup to restore a previously saved configuration. The configuration is saved to a .tgz file. You can store backups locally, or remotely to a TFTP, SCP or FTP server. You can run the backup manually, or do a scheduled backup.
- Save your Gaia system configuration settings as a ready-to-run CLI script. This lets you quickly restore your system configuration after a system failure or migration.

  **Note:** You can only do a migration using the same Gaia version on the source and target computers.

## Backing Up and Restoring the System - WebUI

To add a backup:

1. In the tree view, click Maintenance > System Backup
2. Click Add Backup. The New Backup window opens.
3. Select the location of the backup file:
   - This appliance
   - TFTP server. Specify the IP address.
   - SCP server. Specify the IP address, user name and password.
   - FTP server. Specify the IP address, user name and password.

To restore from a backup:

1. In the tree view, click Maintenance > System Backup.
2. Select the backup file and click Restore Backup.

To delete a backup

1. In the tree view, click Maintenance > System Backup.
2. Select the backup file and click Delete.

## Backing Up and Restoring the System - CLI (Backup)

Backing Up a Configuration

Description: Use these commands to create and save the system's configuration

Syntax:

To create and save a backup locally:

```
add backup local
```

To create and save a backup on a remote server using FTP:

```
add backup ftp ip VALUE username VALUE password plain
```

To create and save a backup on a remote server using TFTP:

```
add backup tftp ip VALUE
```

To save a backup on a remote server using SCP:

```
add backup scp ip VALUE username VALUE password plain
```

Parameters:

| Parameter | Description |
|---|---|
| ip VALUE | The IP address of the remote server. |
| username VALUE | User name required to log in to the remote server. |
| password plain | At the prompt, enter the password for the remote server. |

TABLE 17: Backup

Example

```
add backup local
```

Output

```
gw> add backup local
Creating backup package. Use the command 'show backups' to
monitor creation progress.


gw> show backup status
```

```
Performing local backup

gw> show backups
backup_gw-8b0891_22_7_2012_14_29.tgz Sun, Jul 22, 2012 109.73 MB
```

Comments: Backup configurations are stored in: /var/CPbackup/backups/

### *Restoring a Configuration*

Description: Use these commands to restore the system's configuration from a backup file.

Syntax

To restore a backup from a locally held file:

```
set backup restore local <TAB>
```

To restore a backup from a remote server using FTP:

```
set backup restore ftp ip VALUE file VALUE username VALUE
password plain
```

To restore a backup from a remote server using TFTP:

```
set backup restore tftp ip VALUE file VALUE
```

To restore a backup from a remote server using SCP:

```
set backup restore scp ip VALUE file VALUE username VALUE
password plain
```

Parameters:

| Parameter | Description |
|---|---|
| local <TAB> | The <TAB> does an auto-complete on the name and location of the backup file. |
| ip VALUE | The IP address of the remote server. |
| file VALUE | The location and name of the file on the remote server. |

TABLE 18: Backup Restore

| Parameter | Description |
|---|---|
| username VALUE | User name required to log in to the remote server. |
| password plain | At the prompt, enter the password for the remote server. |

TABLE 18: Backup Restore

Comments: To apply the new configuration, you must reboot.

**Note:** To quickly restore the Gaia OS configuration after a system failure or migration, use the configuration feature.

### *Monitoring Backup Status*

To monitor the creation of a backup:

```
show backup status
```

To show the status of the last backup performed:

```
show backups
```

## Configuring Scheduled Backups - WebUI

1. To add a scheduled backup:
2. In the tree view, click Maintenance > System Backup.
3. Click Add Scheduled Backup. The New Scheduled Backup window opens.
4. In Backup Name, enter the name of the job. Use alphanumeric characters only, and no spaces.
5. In Backup Type, enter the location of the backup file.
    - This appliance
    - TFTP server. Specify the IP address.
    - SCP server. Specify the IP address, user name and password.
    - FTP server. Specify the IP address, user name and password.
6. In Backup Schedule, select the frequency (Daily, Weekly, Monthly) for this backup. Where relevant, enter the Time of day for the job, in the 24 hour clock format.
7. Click Add. The scheduled backup shows in the Scheduled Backups table.

To delete a scheduled backup:

1. In the tree view, click Maintenance > System Backup.
2. In the Scheduled Backups table, select the backup to delete.
3. Click Delete.

## Configuring Scheduled Backups - CLI (backup-scheduled)

Description: Configure a scheduled backup of the system configuration

Syntax

To add a scheduled backup locally:

```
add backup-scheduled name VALUE local
```

To add a scheduled backup on a remote server using FTP:

```
add backup-scheduled name VALUE ftp ip VALUE username
VALUE password plain
```

To add a scheduled backup on a remote server using SCP:

```
add backup-scheduled name VALUE scp ip VALUE username
VALUE password plain
```

To add a scheduled backup on a remote server using TFTP:

```
add backup-scheduled name VALUE tftp ip VALUE
```

To configure a daily backup schedule:

```
set backup-scheduled name VALUE recurrence daily time
VALUE
```

To configure a monthly backup schedule:

```
set backup-scheduled name VALUE recurrence monthly month
VALUE days VALUE time VALUE
```

To configure a weekly backup schedule:

```
set backup-scheduled name VALUE recurrence weekly days
VALUE time VALUE
```

To show the details of the scheduled backup:

```
show backup-scheduled VALUE
```

To delete a scheduled backup:

```
delete backup-scheduled VALUE
```

Parameters:

| Parameter | Description |
|---|---|
| name VALUE | The name of the scheduled backup |
| ip VALUE | The IP address of the FTP, TFTP, or SCP remote server |
| username VALUE | User name required to log in to the remote server |
| backup-scheduled VALUE | The name of a scheduled backup |
| password plain | At the prompt, enter the password for the remote server |
| recurrence daily time | To specify a job for once a day, enter recurrence daily time, and the time of day, in the 24 hour clock format. For example: 14:00 |
| recurrence monthly month | To specify a job for once a month, enter recurrence monthly month, and the specific months. Each month by number, and separate by commas. For example: for January through March, enter:1,2,3 |
| recurrence weekly days | To specify a job for once a week, enter recurrence weekly, and the day by number, when 0 is Sunday and 6 is Saturday. |
| time | To specify the time, enter the time in the twenty four hour clock format. For example: 14:00. |
| days | When the recurrence is weekly: To specify the days, enter the day by number: 0 is Sunday and 6 is Saturday.<br>When the recurrence is monthly: To specify the days, enter the day by number: 1 to 31.<br>Separate several days with commas. For example: for Monday and Thursday enter 1,4 |

TABLE 19: backup-scheduled

## Working with System Configuration - CLI (configuration)

You can save your Gaia system configuration settings as a ready-to-run CLI script. This feature lets you quickly restore your system configuration after a system failure or migration.

> **Note:** You can only do a migration using the same Gaia version on the source and target computers.

To save the system configuration to a CLI Script, run:

```
save configuration <script name>
```

To restore configuration settings, run:

```
load configuration <script name>
<script name> - Name of the script file.
```

To see the latest configuration settings, run:

```
show configuration
```

This example shows part of the configuration settings as last saved to a CLI script:

```
mem103> show configuration
#
# Configuration of mem103
# Language version: 10.0v1
#
# Exported by admin on Mon Mar 19 15:06:22 2012
#
set hostname mem103
set timezone Asia / Jerusalem
set password-controls min-password-length 6
set password-controls complexity 2
set password-controls palindrome-check true
set password-controls history-checking true
set password-controls history-length 10
set password-controls password-expiration never
set ntp active off
```

```
set router-id 6.6.6.103
set ipv6-state off
set snmp agent off
set snmp agent-version any
set snmp community public read-only
set snmp traps trap authorizationError disable
set snmp traps trap coldStart disable
set snmp traps trap configurationChange disable
```

## Emergendisk

Emergendisk is a set of tools on a removable USB device for emergency password recovery and file system access. You can create an Emergendisk removable device that contains these tools:

- **Password recovery** — If you forget your administrator password, you can restore the initial system administrator username and password (admin/admin).
- **System Recovery** — If the Gaia system does not boot up, use the emergendisk tool to boot Gaia from the removable device. You can also use emergendisk to see the file system as it was when Gaia was installed. You can then copy files to the damaged system.
- **Disk Erasure** — Use the DBAN open source tools to securely erase a hard disk. The dban.org site gives this description of the tools: "Darik's Boot and Nuke ("DBAN") is a self-contained boot floppy that securely wipes the hard disks of most computers. DBAN is appropriate for bulk or emergency data destruction."

This is the Emergendisk menu:

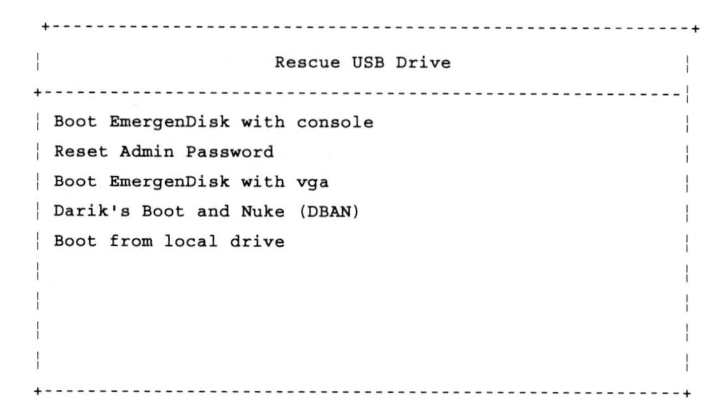

```
+-----------------------------------------------------------+
|                    Rescue USB Drive                        |
+-----------------------------------------------------------|
| Boot EmergenDisk with console                              |
| Reset Admin Password                                       |
| Boot EmergenDisk with vga                                  |
| Darik's Boot and Nuke (DBAN)                               |
| Boot from local drive                                      |
|                                                            |
|                                                            |
|                                                            |
|                                                            |
+-----------------------------------------------------------+

                 Press [Tab] to edit options
```

## Creating the Emergendisk Removable Device

Emergendisk is a set of tools on a removable USB device for emergency password recovery and file system access.

To create the Emergendisk:

1. At the CLI, type expert and then your expert password.
2. Insert a removable device into the USB port on the Gaia computer.
3. Run: emergendisk
4. Choose the removable device. A warning message shows:

   ```
   Warning! all data will be lost from device.
   Are you sure you want to continue [yes/no]?
   ```

5. Type yes. The device is formatted and files are copied. A progress bar shows. After some minutes a success message appears:

   ```
   Emergendisk created successfully
   ```

## Booting from the Emergendisk Removable Device

If the Gaia system does not boot up, use the emergendisk tool to boot Gaia from the removable device. You can also use emergendisk to see the file system as it was when Gaia was installed. You can then copy files to the damaged system.

To boot from the Emergendisk removable device:

1. At the CLI, type expert and then your expert password.
2. Insert the Emergendisk removable device into the USB port on the Gaia computer.
3. Reboot. At the prompt, type

   ```
   reboot
   ```

   The Emergendisk menu displays.
4. Choose one of these options:

   ```
   Boot emergendisk with VGA
   Boot emergendisk with console
   ```

After the reboot, you are in the USB file system. You can see the files system on the Gaia computer in the /mnt/hdd directory.

## Resetting the Administrator Password

If you forget your administrator password, you can restore the initial system administrator username and password (admin/admin).

To reset the administrator password:

1. At the CLI, type expert and then your expert password.
2. Insert the removable device into the USB port on the Gaia computer.
3. At the prompt, type:

   ```
   reboot
   ```

   After the reboot, the Emergendisk menu displays.
4. Choose the option:

   ```
   Reset Admin Password
   ```

   Console messages show. After some minutes, this message shows:

   ```
   Admin password successfully reset
   Please remove disk or any other media and press enter to restart
   ```

5. Remove the removable device from the USB port.
6. Press ENTER to reboot

The default administrator username/password is admin/admin.

## Irrecoverably Erasing Data using DBAN

Use the DBAN open source tools to securely erase a hard disk. The dban.org site gives this description of the tools: "Darik's Boot and Nuke ("DBAN") is a self-contained boot floppy that securely wipes the hard disks of most computers. DBAN is appropriate for bulk or emergency data destruction."

To Erase the Disk of the DBAN tools:

1. At the CLI, type expert and then your expert password.
2. Insert the removable device into the USB port on the Gaia computer with the disk to erase.
3. At the prompt, type

   **`reboot`**

4. After the reboot, the Emergendisk menu opens.
5. Choose the option:

   **`Darik's Boot and Nuke (DBAN)`**

6. The DBAN menu shows the different ways of erasing the disk:

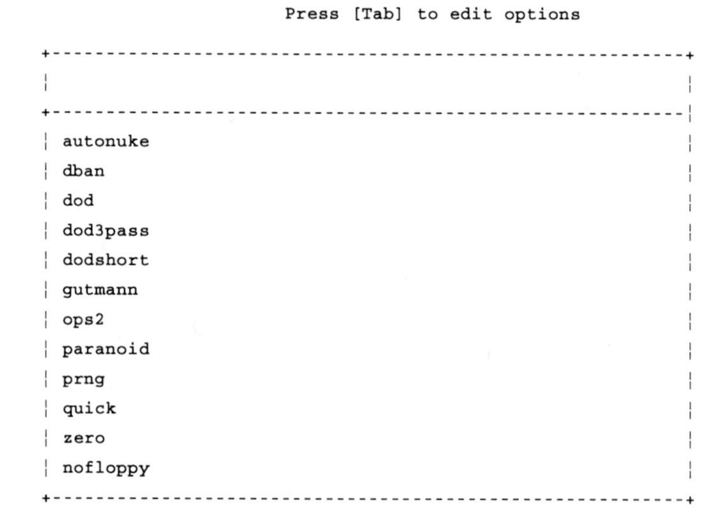

Press [Tab] to edit options
autonuke
dban
dod
dod3pass
dodshort
gutmann
ops2
paranoid
prng
quick
zero
nofloppy


Choose the appropriate option.

## Typical Troubleshooting Resolution

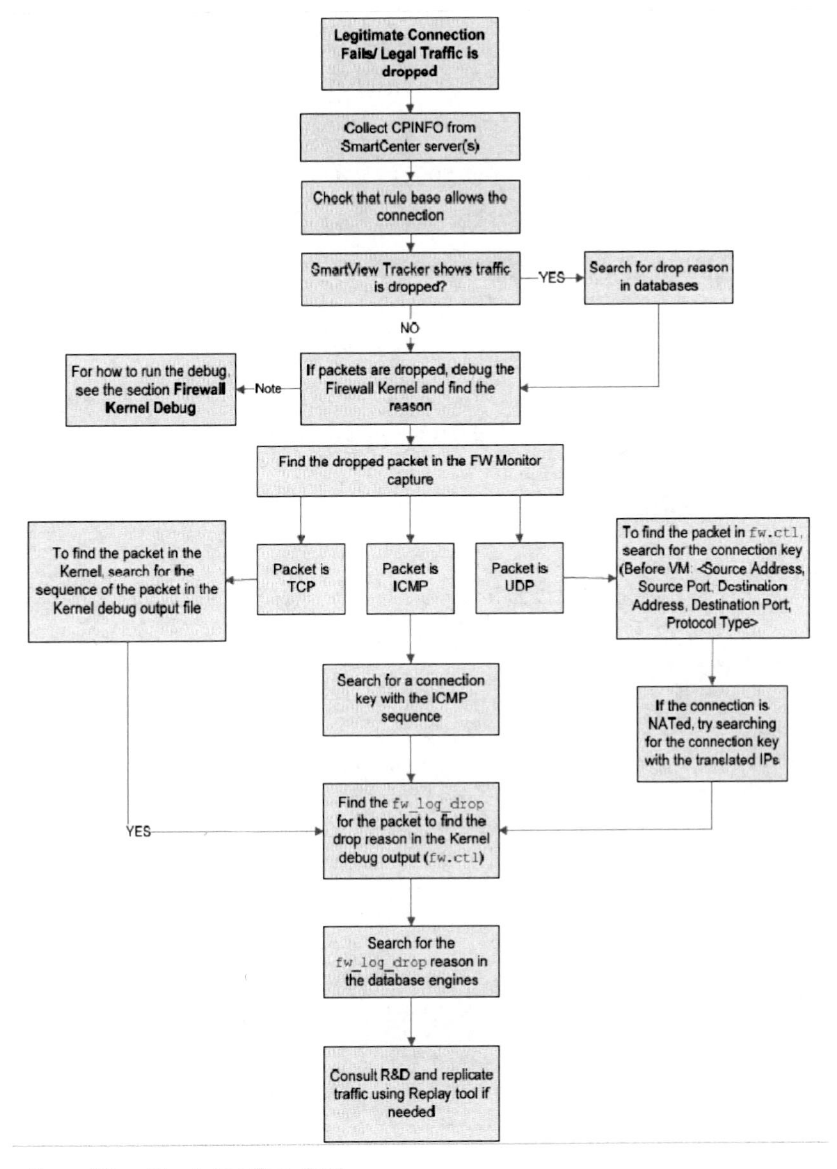


Figure 50 — Resolution Flowchart

Always search for the drop reason in the database engines.

- Refer to the Release Notes and guides for support for special protocols.

## *Firewall Kernel Debug*

The following is the general Kernel debug that should be suitable for most situations. (If a more thorough debug of the Kernel modules is required, you can see the full list of the modules by running fw ctl debug –h on the Gateway.)

```
# fw monitor -e "accept;" -o log.out
# fw ctl debug 0
# fw ctl debug -buf 8192
# fw ctl debug -m fw + drop conn
# fw ctl kdebug -f > fw.ctl
// Replicate dropped
#fw ctl debug 0
# kill monitor with CTRL+C
```

APPENDIX B

# Chapter Questions and Answers

# *Chapter 1 - Advanced Upgrading*

1. When should snapshots be performed?

   *At least once, and before major changes, such as upgrades*

2. To run advanced upgrade or migration, what tool is used?

   *migrate.*

3. What is a critical task for both Snapshots and Backups?

   *Testing your backups with either the backup, upgrade_export, or migrate export files.*

# Chapter 2 - Advanced Firewall

1. The core process CPD allows provides what main functions?

   *SIC (Secure Internal Communication) functionality – ports 18xxx are used for this communication*

   *Status – pull AMON status from the GW/Management using SmartEvent Transferring messages between FW-1 processes.*

   *Policy installation – received the policy (on the GW) and pushes it forward to relevant processes and the Kernel*

2. The firewall's kernel consists of two completely separate logical parts representing the process of a packet coming into and out from the firewall, these are referred to as...

   *Inbound and Outbound*

# *Chapter 3 - Clustering and Acceleration*

1. What is the main advantage of Monitored-circuit VRRP??

   *Eliminates "black holes" caused by asymmetric routes when one interface on the master fails*

2. What two modes does State Synchronization work in?

   *Full synchronization, Delta synchronization*

3. What does Checkpoint recommend for securing the synchronization interfaces?

   *Using a dedicated sync network, or connecting the physical network interfaces of the cluster members directly using a cross-over cable.*

4. In a Management HA environment, how do you know when the Secondary SMS ready?

   *It is represented on the Primary SMS by a network object.*

   *SIC has been initialized between it and the Primary SMS.*

   *Manual synchronization has been completed with the Primary SMS for the first time.*

# *Chapter 4 - Advanced User Management*

1. What objects make up an Organizational Unit container?

   *Resources, Services, Users*

2. What does an LDAP Schema do?

   *Defines the types of objects and object attributes in the directory*

3. How long can it take for an AD Query to map users and computers to IPs?

   *AD Query may take up to a few hours to complete the mapping of users and computers to IPs.*

4. If you cannot connect to the source IP **C$** share or with WMI Explorer, what is the likely cause?

   *This IP is a computer that is not a member of the domain.*

## *Chapter 5 - Advanced IPsec VPN and Remote Access*

1. What are the stages of a Phase 2 IKE exchange?

   *Peers exchange more key material, and agree on encryption and integrity methods for IPSec.*

   *The DH key is combined with the key material to produce the symmetrical IPSec key.*

   *Symmetric IPSec keys are generated.*

2. What is the advantage of Link Selection for VPN traffic?

   *When high-traffic demands are applied to the gateway and its performance is impaired, Link Selection provides the means to specify which interfaces are to be used for incoming and outgoing VPN traffic*

3. What type of VPN communities can be explicitly defined as MEP VPNs?

   *Only Star VPN Communities using more than one central Security Gateway can be defined explicitly as MEP VPNs.*

4. Quick mode packet 1 fails with error "No Proposal Chosen" from the peer. What is likely the cause?

   *This failure is usually caused when a peer does not agree to the proposal fields, such as encryption strength or hash.*

# Chapter 6 - Auditing and Reporting

1. What does the SmartReporter Consolidation Policy do?

   *The Consolidation Policy goes over your original, "raw" log file, compressing similar events and writing the compressed list of events into a relational database.*

2. What is the difference between a Consolidation Policy, and a Security Policy?

   *A Consolidation Policy is based on logs, as opposed to connections, and has no bearing on security issues.*

3. When is an event reported?

   *When created*

   *Up to five updates*

   *When it is closed*